From our Kitchen to Yours

ALL-TIME-FAVORITE RECIPES
From

COLORADO

Dedication

For every cook who wants to create amazing
recipes from the great state of Colorado.

Appreciation

Thanks to all our Colorado cooks who shared their
delightful and delicious recipes with us!

Gooseberry Patch
An imprint of Globe Pequot
246 Goose Lane
Guilford, CT 06437
www.gooseberrypatch.com
1 800 854 6673

Copyright 2020, Gooseberry Patch
978-162093-395-4

Do you have a tried & true recipe, tip, craft or
memory that you'd like to see featured in a
Gooseberry Patch cookbook? Visit our website at
www.gooseberrypatch.com and follow the easy steps
to submit your favorite family recipe.

Or send them to us at:

Gooseberry Patch
PO Box 812
Columbus, OH 43216-0812

Don't forget to include the number of servings your
recipe makes, plus your name, address, phone
number and email address. If we select your recipe,
your name will appear right along with it...and you'll
receive a FREE copy of the book!

COLORADO COOKS

ICONIC COLORADO

Colorful Colorado was originally settled by Spanish explorers and comprised of four different territories. Each of these territories offered a variety of vast landscapes that has provided Colorado with a history of diverse agricultural opportunities and foods.

From the highest mountains to the lowest plains...plentiful for farming and ranching and forests with rivers running through, abundant with fresh fish...Colorado is known for some of the most amazing recipes. Colorado recipes often feature bison, lamb, fish, melon, sweet corn and peaches. Many of these recipes are made with Mexican spices and have Spanish flair due to the influence of Spanish settlers.

Although the Gold Rush is over, today Colorado maintains a strong reputation for large production agriculture. It is a leading producer of market-fresh products, winter wheat, dairy production and ranching of cattle and sheep.

The amazing cooks from the Centennial State have shared recipes that are dear to their hearts. You'll find everything from Jalapeño Popper Dip and Colorado Ski Chili Bake to Oxtail Soup and Pork Tenderloin with Roasted Grapes. We know you will love this collection of tried & true recipes from cooks from all around the great state of Colorado. Enjoy!

OUR STORY

Back in 1984, our families were neighbors in little Delaware, Ohio. With small children, we wanted to do what we loved and stay home with the kids too. We had always shared a love of home cooking and so, **Gooseberry Patch** was born.

Almost immediately, we found a connection with our customers and it wasn't long before these friends started sharing recipes. Since then we've enjoyed publishing hundreds of cookbooks with your tried & true recipes.

We know we couldn't have done it without our friends all across the country and we look forward to continuing to build a community with you. Welcome to the **Gooseberry Patch** family!

JoAnn & Vickie

TABLE OF CONTENTS

CHAPTER ONE

Prairie-Perfect

Breakfast

ENJOY THESE TASTY BREAKFAST
RECIPES THAT BRING YOU TO THE
TABLE WITH A HEARTY "GOOD
MORNING!" AND CARRY YOU
THROUGH THE DAY TO TACKLE
WHATEVER COMES YOUR WAY.

BANANA-OAT BREAKFAST COOKIES

SANDRA SULLIVAN
AURORA, CO

Need something new for breakfast? These satisfying cookies are great with a glass of cold milk or a cup of hot coffee.

1/2 c. ripe bananas, mashed

1/2 c. crunchy peanut butter

1/2 c. honey

1 t. vanilla extract

1 c. quick-cooking oats, uncooked

1/2 c. whole-wheat flour

1/4 c. powdered milk

2 t. cinnamon

1/4 t. baking soda

1 c. sweetened dried cranberries or raisins

In a large bowl, stir together bananas, peanut butter, honey and vanilla; set aside. In a small bowl, combine oats, flour, powdered milk, cinnamon and baking soda. Add oat mixture to banana mixture; stir until blended. Fold in cranberries or raisins. Lightly coat 2 baking sheets with non-stick vegetable spray. Drop mounds of dough onto baking sheets by 1/4 cupfuls, 3 inches apart. With a spatula dipped in water, flatten each mound into a 2-3/4 inch circle, about 1/2-inch thick. Bake at 350 degrees, one sheet at a time, for 14 to 16 minutes, until golden. Transfer cookies to wire racks to cool. Store in an airtight container up to 3 days. Cookies may also be cooled, wrapped and frozen; thaw before serving.

Makes one dozen

SLOW-COOKED
GREEN EGGS & HAM

APRIL JACOBS
LOVELAND, CO

This dish is named after one of my son's favorite books. It's one of the few ways I can get him to eat spinach, so I'm glad he likes it. We'll sometimes stir this up for dinner too.

In a bowl, whisk together eggs, milk, yogurt and seasonings until smooth. Stir in mushrooms, spinach, cheese and ham. Spoon egg mixture into a lightly greased slow cooker. Cover and cook on high setting for 1-1/2 to 2 hours, until eggs are set. Sprinkle servings with Parmesan cheese, if desired.

Serves 6

6 eggs
1/4 c. milk
1/2 c. plain Greek yogurt
1/2 t. dried thyme
1/2 t. onion powder
1/2 t. garlic powder
1/2 t. salt
1/4 t. pepper
1/3 c. mushrooms, diced
1 c. baby spinach
1 c. shredded Pepper Jack cheese
1 c. cooked ham, diced
Optional: grated Parmesan cheese

WESTERN OMELET CASEROLE

VICKIE
GOOSEBERRY PATCH

*Is there anything as tasty as a Western omelet? The crisp pepper,
salty ham and melty cheese...mmmm! Makes my mouth water just
thinking about it.*

**32-oz. pkg. frozen
shredded hashbrowns**
1 lb. cooked ham, cubed
1 green pepper, diced
1/2 onion, chopped
**1-1/2 c. shredded
Cheddar cheese**
1 doz. eggs
1 c. milk
1 t. salt
1 t. pepper

Layer 1/3 each of potatoes, ham, green pepper,
onion and cheese in a slow cooker. Repeat layering
2 more times, ending with cheese. In a bowl, beat
together eggs, milk, salt and pepper. Pour over
mixture in slow cooker. Cover and cook on low
setting for 8 to 10 hours, until a toothpick inserted
near the center tests clean.

Serves 8 to 10

COLORADO FUN FACT

The Dwight Eisenhower Memorial Tunnel
between Clear Creek & Summit counties is
the highest auto tunnel in the world. Bored
at an elevation of 11,000 feet under the
Continental Divide, it is 8,960 feet long and
the average daily traffic exceeds 26,000
vehicles.

MEXICAN BREAKFAST CASEROLE

RITA MORGAN
PUEBLO, CO

I first tried this recipe when I was planning a church breakfast potluck...it was a hit! Now I serve it often.

Spray a large slow cooker well with non-stick vegetable spray. Arrange 3 tortillas to cover the bottom of slow cooker, tearing to fit as needed; set aside. Reserve 2 tablespoons red pepper, 2 tablespoons green onions and 3/4 cup cheese; refrigerate. To slow cooker, add half of sausage and half each of remaining red pepper, green onions and cheese. Add 3 more tortillas, torn to fit; repeat layers. Top with remaining tortillas, tearing as needed to cover mixture. In a large bowl, whisk together eggs, milk and chiles; pour mixture over top. Cover and cook on low setting for 4 to 5 hours, or on high setting for 2 to 3 hours, until set in the center. Top with reserved cheese, pepper and onions; add cilantro. Serve with salsa.

Serves 6

9 taco-size corn tortillas, divided
1 red pepper, diced and divided
3/4 c. green onions, sliced and divided
8-oz. pkg. shredded Mexican-blend cheese, divided
1 lb. ground breakfast sausage, browned, drained and divided
8 eggs
1-1/2 c. milk
1 T. canned diced green chiles, drained
1 to 2 T. fresh cilantro, chopped
Garnish: salsa

SAUSAGE & CHERRY TART WITH WALNUTS

SHARON DEMERS
DOLORES, CO

This tart is perfect for brunches and teas. The combination of flavors is wonderful!

1 c. all-purpose flour
2/3 c. walnuts, ground
1 T. sugar
1/4 t. salt
1/2 t. dry mustard
1/8 t. cayenne pepper
6 T. chilled butter, cubed
1 to 2 T. milk
1/2 lb. ground pork
   breakfast sausage
1 onion, finely diced
1/2 to 1 c. dried tart
   cherries or cranberries
1/2 c. chopped walnuts
1/4 t. dried thyme
2 eggs, beaten
1 c. whipping cream
3-oz. pkg. crumbled
   Gorgonzola cheese

Combine flour, ground walnuts, sugar, salt, mustard, cayenne pepper and butter in a food processor. Pulse just until mixture resembles bread crumbs. Add one tablespoon milk; pulse until dough comes together. If dough is too crumbly, add more milk until it holds together. Shape dough into a ball and press evenly into a lightly greased 9" round tart pan. Freeze for 30 minutes. Bake crust at 350 degrees for 15 to 20 minutes, or until golden. Remove from oven and set aside. Brown sausage and onion in a skillet over medium heat; drain well. Stir in cherries or cranberries, walnuts and thyme. Set aside. Combine eggs and cream; whisk until smooth. Spoon sausage mixture into baked crust; sprinkle with cheese. Pour egg mixture over all. Bake at 350 degrees for 15 to 20 minutes, or until golden and center tests done. Cool 15 minutes before serving.

Serves 8

ORANGE-CINNAMON FRENCH TOAST

DEBRA FLEISCHACKER
AURORA, CO

Good recipes always get passed along, as this one will!

Combine butter, honey and cinnamon together in a lightly greased 13"x9" baking pan and set aside. Blend eggs, orange juice and salt together. Dip bread slices into egg mixture, coating both sides. Arrange dipped bread slices in baking pan. Bake, uncovered, at 400 degrees for 15 to 20 minutes, until golden.

Serves 3 to 4

2 to 4 T. butter, melted
2 T. honey
1/2 t. cinnamon
3 eggs, beaten
1/2 c. frozen orange juice concentrate, partially thawed
1/8 t. salt
6 slices French bread

BONUS IDEA

Save the memories! Be sure to take pictures at your gathering and share copies with friends as a thank-you for coming. Or use an instant camera for added fun...give pictures to guests on their way home.

DILLED CRAB EGG CUPS

**SANDRA SULLIVAN
AURORA, CO**

A great dish for pop-up brunches and get-togethers.

1/2 lb. crabmeat, flaked

8-oz. pkg. cream cheese, diced

1 T. fresh dill, chopped and divided

1 doz. eggs

1/2 c. milk

1/2 c. sour cream

Optional: salad greens, favorite-flavor salad dressing

Divide crabmeat and cream cheese evenly among 12 greased muffin cups. Sprinkle dill into each cup. In a bowl, whisk together eggs, milk and sour cream. Divide egg mixture among muffin cups, filling each about 3/4 full. Bake at 450 degrees for 10 to 15 minutes, until puffed and golden. Cool slightly; remove from tin. Serve egg cups on a bed of salad greens drizzled with dressing, if desired.

Makes one dozen

KITCHEN TIP

A crock of honey butter...so yummy on warm bread, biscuits and muffins. Simply blend together 1/2 cup each of honey and softened butter.

MAPLE-WALNUTTY SPREAD

SHARON DEMERS
DOLORES, CO

Perfect to spread on piping-hot scones in the fall.

Beat cream cheese with syrup and extract until well mixed. Fold in walnuts. Let stand 20 to 30 minutes to allow flavors to blend before serving. Keep refrigerated.

Makes about 1-1/2 cups.

8-oz. pkg. cream cheese, softened

2 T. maple syrup

1/2 t. maple extract

1/2 c. chopped walnuts, toasted

MOCHA MUFFINS

PAIGE WOODARD
LOVELAND, CO

I first tasted these muffins at a brunch given by my mother, and knew right away that my husband would love them! I was right...topped with a creamy spread, they've become a must-have at all of our family brunches.

Whisk together flour, sugar, baking powder, cinnamon and salt in a large bowl. In a small bowl, stir milk and 2 tablespoons coffee granules until coffee is dissolved. Add butter, egg and vanilla; mix well. Stir into flour mixture just until moistened. Fold in 3/4 cup chocolate chips. Fill greased or paper-lined muffin cups 2/3 full. Bake at 375 degrees for 17 to 20 minutes for regular muffins, or 13 to 15 minutes for mini muffins. Cool for 5 minutes before removing from pans to wire racks. In a food processor or blender, combine cream cheese and remaining vanilla, coffee granules and mini chocolate chips. Cover and process until well blended. Refrigerate spread until serving time. Serve spread on the side.

Makes 16 regular muffins

2 c. all-purpose flour

3/4 c. plus 1 T. sugar

2-1/2 t. baking powder

1 t. cinnamon

1/2 t. salt

1 c. milk

2 T. plus 1/2 t. instant coffee granules, divided

1/2 c. butter, melted

1 egg, beaten

1-1/2 t. vanilla extract, divided

1 c. mini semi-sweet chocolate chips, divided

1/2 c. cream cheese, softened

OVERNIGHT OMELET CASSEROLE

JO ANN
GOOSEBERRY PATCH

Delicious and so simple to put together. Great for a sunrise brunch or for anytime you have overnight guests.

12 slices white bread, crusts trimmed

2 to 4 T. butter, softened

6 slices American cheese

2/3 c. cooked ham, diced

1 green pepper, diced

1 onion, diced

2 c. shredded Swiss cheese

1 doz. eggs

1-1/2 c. milk

6 to 8 slices Canadian bacon

Spread both sides of bread slices with butter. Line the bottom of an ungreased 13"x9" baking pan with 6 slices; top each slice with a cheese slice. Sprinkle with ham, green pepper and onion. Arrange remaining bread slices on top; sprinkle with Swiss cheese. Whisk together eggs and milk in a bowl; pour over cheese. Cover and refrigerate overnight. Just before baking, arrange Canadian bacon slices on top. Bake, uncovered, at 400 degrees for 10 minutes. Reduce heat to 375 degrees; bake for an additional 50 minutes, or until eggs are set and cheese is melted.

Serves 8

MA CARRICO'S
BUTTERMILK PANCAKES

SHEILA COPE
COLORADO SPRINGS, CO

These pancakes are the best! I got this recipe from Irene Carrico, who has since passed away, while I was working for her at the Arctic Circle Restaurant in Kanab, Utah. "Ma" made these for me every morning...sometimes she would spoil me by adding mashed bananas to the batter and drizzling strawberry syrup over the top.

Combine all ingredients; mix well. Pour by 1/4 cupfuls on a hot griddle sprayed with non-stick vegetable spray over medium heat. Cook pancakes until golden and bubbles appear around edges; flip and cook other side.

Makes 12 to 15, 4-inch pancakes

1 c. all-purpose flour
1 t. baking powder
1/4 t. baking soda
1/2 t. salt
1 c. buttermilk
1 egg, beaten
3 T. sugar
3 T. oil

COUNTRY CABIN PANCAKE SYRUP

RITA MORGAN
PUEBLO, CO

Slip a jar of this delectable syrup into a basket along with some pancake mix...a welcome surprise for neighbors.

2 16-oz. pkg's. dark brown sugar
1 c. sugar
1/2 t. salt
4 c. water
3/4 c. corn syrup
1 T. maple extract

Combine all ingredients except extract in a saucepan. Bring to a boil over medium heat; boil for about 10 minutes, stirring constantly, until sugars are dissolved and mixture is thickened. Let cool to lukewarm; stir in extract. Place in a covered container; keep refrigerated for up to 4 weeks.

Makes 7 cups

BACON-MUSHROOM FRITTATA

APRIL JACOBS
LOVELAND, CO

I've been buying fresh eggs from the same lady at our neighborhood farmers' market for over 15 years now! With country-style bacon and fresh herbs, this frittata is an extra-special breakfast.

In a cast-iron skillet over medium heat, cook bacon until crisp. Drain bacon on paper towels. Add mushrooms and onion to drippings in skillet. Cook for about 5 minutes, until mushrooms are golden and onion is translucent; drain and remove from heat. In a separate bowl, whisk together eggs, sour cream, seasonings and mushroom mixture. Pour egg mixture into same skillet or a lightly greased 9" pie plate. Sprinkle evenly with crumbled bacon. Bake at 425 degrees for 15 minutes. Reduce heat to 300 degrees; bake an additional 10 minutes, or until eggs are completely set. Remove from oven. Sprinkle with cheese; let stand 5 minutes. Slice into wedges; serve warm.

Makes 4 to 6 servings

8 slices bacon, crisply cooked and crumbled

2 c. sliced mushrooms

1 c. onion, chopped

6 eggs, beaten

3/4 c. sour cream

1 t. fresh oregano, chopped

salt and pepper to taste

1/3 c. shredded Cheddar cheese

GRANDFATHER'S DUTCH BREAD

BARBARA HIGHTOWER
BROOMFIELD, CO

We have a family tradition of Dutch Bread for Christmas morning breakfast, and now, so do my own children and their families. Christmas just wouldn't be Christmas without it!

16-oz. pkg. hot roll mix
1 c. hot water
2 T. butter, softened
3 eggs, divided
1 c. half-and-half
1/8 t. salt
2/3 c. sugar
cinnamon to taste
Garnish: sliced butter

In a large bowl, combine hot roll mix and yeast packet from mix; stir well. Heat water until very warm, about 120 to 130 degrees. Add water, butter and one egg to roll mix. Stir well until a soft dough forms; form into a ball. Knead dough on a floured surface for 5 minutes, or until smooth. Cover dough with a large bowl; let stand for 5 minutes. Divide dough in half. Roll one half into an 8-inch circle; place in a greased 8" round cake pan. Repeat with other half. Cover pans with tea towels. Let stand in a warm place until dough rises a little above the top of the pans, about 30 to 45 minutes. Make indentations, one inch apart, in both pans of dough with a floured thumb. Whisk together remaining eggs, half-and-half and salt; pour mixture evenly into indentations from a measuring cup with a spout. Sprinkle evenly with sugar and cinnamon; dot with butter. Bake at 375 degrees for 15 to 20 minutes, until tops are lightly golden and custard is set. Bread may be baked the night before, refrigerated and warmed in the morning.

Makes 2 loaves

CHILI RELLENOS CASSEROLE

CHANELLE REY
ORDWAY, CO

We love chili rellenos, but stuffing the individual chiles is a lot of fuss. This yummy recipe goes together in a jiffy!

Layer chiles and cheese slices in a greased 13"x9" baking pan; set aside. Whisk together eggs, flour, milk, shortening and salt; mix well and pour over cheese. Bake, uncovered, at 350 degrees for 30 minutes, or until golden.

Serves 6 to 8

2 8-oz. cans whole green chiles, drained
1 lb. Monterey Jack cheese, sliced
6 eggs, beaten
1-1/2 c. all-purpose flour
2 c. milk
3 T. shortening, melted and slightly cooled
1/4 t. salt

DINNERTIME CONVERSATION

Did you know the Denver Mint produced 15.4 billion coins in fiscal year 2000, more coins than ever produced by a single U.S. Mint facility? The mint celebrated its 100th anniversary of coin production in 2006.

STRAWBERRY-THYME JAM

SHARON DEMERS
DOLORES, CO

I love the taste of strawberries and fresh thyme, and this is a refreshing jam that's oh-so good on buttermilk scones or hot biscuits.

4 pts. fresh
  strawberries, hulled
  and crushed
1 T. fresh thyme,
  chopped
1-3/4 oz. pkg. powdered
  fruit pectin
Optional: 1/2 t. butter
7 c. sugar
8 1/2-pint canning jars
  and lids, sterilized

Place strawberries into a large stockpot; add thyme. Stir in pectin and mix well. Add butter, if using, to reduce foaming. Bring mixture to a rolling boil over high heat, stirring constantly. Add sugar all at once. Return to a rolling boil; boil for one minute. Remove from heat; skim off foam. Spoon into hot sterilized jars, leaving 1/4-inch headspace. Wipe rims; secure with lids and rings. Process in a boiling water bath for 10 minutes. Set jars on a towel to cool completely; check for seals.

Makes 7 to 8 jars

FEEL-GOOD SHAKE

PATTI BOEPPLE
TRINIDAD, CO

This shake is a perfect way to start your day. One sip and you'll be hooked.

2 bananas, sliced
2 c. milk
2 c. non-fat vanilla
  yogurt
1 c. pineapple juice
1 T. honey

Process all ingredients together in a blender until smooth. Pour into a tall glass. Serve immediately.

Makes one serving

STUFFED FRENCH TOAST

**CINDA LASINSKI
CENTENNIAL, CO**

I began making this recipe for my family years ago for our traditional Christmas morning brunch. It was such a huge success that I decided to make it every year. By changing the pie filling, I have a new recipe each time. It's easy to make and my grandchildren absolutely love it...the adults do too!

Spread half of the bread cubes in a greased 13"x9" baking pan. Scatter cream cheese cubes over bread. If using 2 cans pie filling, partially drain. Spoon pie filling evenly over cream cheese. Top with remaining bread. In a bowl, whisk together remaining ingredients; pour over bread and cheese. Cover and refrigerate overnight. Bake at 375 degrees for 45 minutes, or until hot and eggs are set.

Serves 10 to 12

8 thick slices Italian bread, cubed and divided

2 8-oz. pkgs. reduced-fat cream cheese, cubed

1 to 2 21-oz. cans light cherry, blueberry or peach pie filling

1 doz. eggs, beaten, or equivalent egg substitute

2 c. skim milk

1/3 c. pure maple syrup

1/8 t. nutmeg or cinnamon

CHAPTER TWO

Pikes' Mile–High

Salads & Sides

TOSS TOGETHER GREAT TASTE AND
HEALTHY GOODNESS TO MAKE
FRESH, SATISFYING AND TASTY
SALADS THAT ARE PACKED WITH
FULL–ON FLAVOR.

BRENDA'S FAMOUS GREEN CHILE POTATOES

BRENDA SCHLOSSER
BRIGHTON, CO

I created this potato recipe 15 years ago when I worked for the phone company in Sacramento. I took it often to potlucks...I could hardly get in the door before I was attacked by people wanting some at 8 a.m.! You don't even have to peel the potatoes.

4 to 5 baking potatoes, thinly sliced and divided

garlic powder, salt and pepper to taste

12-oz. container sour cream, divided

1 to 1-1/2 c. canned roasted green chiles

6 green onions, chopped

1 lb. bacon, crisply cooked and crumbled

2 c. shredded Cheddar cheese

1 T. Worcestershire sauce

1/4 c. butter, sliced

Arrange half of potato slices, slightly overlapping, in a greased 13"x9" baking pan. Sprinkle with seasonings; spread half of sour cream over potatoes. Layer with chiles, remaining sour cream, onions, bacon, cheese, remaining potatoes, additional seasonings and Worcestershire sauce. Dot with butter. Cover with aluminum foil. Bake at 375 degrees for 60 to 75 minutes, until potatoes are tender.

Serves 8 to 10

PENNE WITH KALE & ONION

SANDRA SULLIVAN
AURORA, CO

We didn't think we liked kale until I swapped it for the spinach in this yummy recipe. But you can always use spinach if you wish.

In a large skillet over medium heat, cook onion in one tablespoon oil for 15 to 20 minutes, or until golden. Add garlic during the last 2 minutes of cook time. In a large stockpot filled with boiling water, cook pasta according to package directions; drain and drizzle with remaining oil. In a Dutch oven, bring one inch of water to a boil and add kale. Cover and cook for 10 to 15 minutes, until tender; drain. Stir salt, pasta and kale into onion mixture and heat through.

1 onion, sliced
2 T. olive oil, divided
8 cloves garlic, thinly sliced
3 c. penne pasta, uncooked
6 c. kale, chopped
1/2 t. salt

Serves 6

MOM'S YUMMY CORNBREAD SALAD

DENISE NEAL
CASTLE ROCK, CO

Because this salad disappears so quickly when I serve it at summer get-togethers, I usually double the recipe! Mom was a great cook, and it makes me feel close to her when I prepare her recipes. When I compiled a family cookbook recently, this recipe was a must-have.

1 c. cornbread, coarsely crumbled

8-3/4 oz. can corn, drained

1/2 c. green onions, chopped

1/2 c. cucumber, chopped

1/2 c. broccoli, chopped

1/2 c. red pepper, chopped

1/2 c. tomato, chopped

1/2 c. canned pinto or garbanzo beans, drained and rinsed

1/2 c. shredded Cheddar cheese

1/2 c. buttermilk ranch salad dressing

salt and pepper to taste

Combine all ingredients in a large bowl, adding salt and pepper to taste. Gently mix and cover. Best when refrigerated for at least 4 hours before serving.

Serves 6

FETA CHEESE TOSSED SALAD

HOLLY CHILD
PARKER, CO

This simple salad is packed with a lot of flavor, thanks to the feta cheese and walnuts.

In a salad bowl, combine all ingredients except oil and vinegar. Toss to mix. Drizzle oil and vinegar over salad; toss again. Cover and refrigerate for at least one hour. Serve chilled.

Serves 4 to 6

- 1 head green leaf lettuce, torn into bite-size pieces
- 8-oz. container crumbled feta cheese
- 3/4 c. chopped walnuts
- 3 to 4 stalks celery, finely chopped
- 1/2 t. pepper
- 2 T. oil
- 2 T. white vinegar

KITCHEN TIP

A crispy salad or chilled fruit is so nice served alongside a bowl of steaming soup. Just for fun, spoon salad or fruit into hollowed-out tomato halves, or line berry pails with leaf lettuce and then spoon inside. So pretty on a buffet table!

SPINACH, STRAWBERRY & WALNUT SALAD

CHERYL DONNELLY
ARVADA, CO

One of the emergency medical technicians I work with made this salad one night for dinner, and several of us asked for the recipe. It's so simple, but combined, the flavor is amazing!

1-1/2 lbs. spinach, torn

3 c. strawberries, hulled and sliced

1 sweet onion, thinly sliced

1 c. chopped walnuts

POPPY SEED DRESSING

3/4 c. sugar

1 t. dry mustard

1 t. salt

1/3 c. cider vinegar

2 t. green onion, chopped

3/4 to 1 c. olive oil

1-1/2 T. poppy seed

Arrange spinach, strawberries, onions and nuts in a salad bowl. Cover and refrigerate. At serving time, drizzle desired amount of Poppy Seed Dressing over salad. Toss and serve immediately.

Poppy Seed Dressing: In a blender, mix sugar, mustard, salt and vinegar until smooth. Add onion and blend until smooth. With blender running, add oil slowly. Blend until thick. Stir in poppy seed.

Serves 6

GINGERED SHRIMP & SNOW PEAS

SANDRA SULLIVAN
AURORA, CO

A flavorful salad that's a meal in itself!

Place a steamer basket in a large saucepan; fill pan with water and bring to a boil. Add snow peas; cover and cook for 2 minutes. Remove basket, reserving boiling water in saucepan; transfer peas to a bowl of ice water to cool. Drain peas and pat dry; cut on the diagonal into1/2-inch pieces. Add shrimp directly to boiling water; return to a boil and cook for 2 minutes. Drain shrimp; plunge into a bowl of ice water. Drain and pat dry; slice shrimp in half lengthwise. In a large bowl, toss shrimp, peas, radishes and onions together. In a smaller bowl, whisk vinegar, oils and ginger; add salt to taste. Drizzle vinegar mixture over salad; toss salad and top with sesame seed.

Serves 4

3/4 lb. snow peas, trimmed
1-1/4 lbs. medium shrimp, cleaned
6 radishes, thinly sliced
4 green onions, thinly sliced
1/3 c. vinegar
1 T. canola oil
1 T. toasted sesame oil
1 T. fresh ginger, peeled and grated
salt to taste
2 T. toasted sesame seed

TRIED & TRUE
CRANBERRY SALAD

KAREN SYLVIA
BRIGHTON, CO

This recipe was made by my grandmother, my mother and my aunt..now I'm the one making it each holiday.

- 16-oz. can whole-berry cranberry sauce
- 8-oz. can crushed pineapple, drained
- 8-oz. container frozen whipped topping, thawed
- 8-oz. container sour cream

Mix all ingredients together in a large bowl. Spoon into a 9"x5" loaf pan lined with aluminum foil. Freeze for 24 hours. Slice and serve immediately.

Serves 18

COLORADO FUN FACT

You can be in Colorado, Arizona, New Mexico and Utah all at the same time! Colorado's southwest corner borders Arizona, New Mexico and Utah and is the only place in America where the corners of four states meet.

BEANS SOUTHWESTERN STYLE

TERESA GRIMSLEY
ALAMOSA, CO

I've developed this recipe over time, and it is absolutely the best bean recipe I've ever had! It's perfect with a big piece of cornbread after a chilly day of snowshoeing.

Combine broth, vegetables, tomatoes with juice, garlic and cumin in a slow cooker. Add beans and pork to broth mixture. Cover and cook on low setting for 8 hours, until beans are tender and pork pulls apart easily. Remove pork from slow cooker and shred; set aside. Using a blender or immersion blender, purée about half of the beans and liquid mixture. Spoon pork back into slow cooker; mix well. Top servings with cilantro, salsa and sour cream, if desired.

Serves 8 to 10

6 c. low-sodium chicken broth
1 onion, chopped
2 T. diced green chiles
1 carrot, peeled and chopped
1 stalk celery, chopped
14-1/2 oz. can diced tomatoes
4 cloves garlic, finely chopped
1 T. ground cumin
3 c. dried pinto beans
1 c. dried black beans
1-1/2 lb. pork shoulder roast
Garnish: chopped fresh cilantro, salsa verde
Optional: sour cream

SWISS-ONION CASEROLE

DOLORES MCCURRY
PUEBLO, CO

My mother-in-law gave me this recipe many years ago. It's always a big hit when I take it to church suppers and other events...a delicious side dish that goes with just about anything.

6 onions, sliced

1/2 c. plus 3 T. butter, softened and divided

10-oz. pkg. shredded Swiss cheese

10-3/4 oz. can cream of mushroom with roasted garlic soup

1/2 c. milk

1 t. soy sauce

pepper to taste

12 to 15 slices baguette bread, sliced 1/2-inch thick

In a skillet over medium heat, sauté onions in 2 to 3 tablespoons butter until tender. Spread in a lightly greased 13"x9" baking pan. Cover with cheese; set aside. In a saucepan over medium heat, stir together soup, milk, soy sauce and pepper. Heat until bubbly; spoon over cheese. Spread remaining butter over both sides of bread. Arrange bread on top of casserole. Bake, uncovered, at 350 degrees for 30 minutes.

Serves 10

SAVORY BEANS & TOMATOES OVER RICE

JEWELL ULRICH
COLORADO SPRINGS, CO

This delicious meal is just minutes away...packed with flavor and so satisfying!

In a large skillet over medium heat, cook bacon until crisp. Remove bacon to a plate and keep warm, reserving drippings in pan. Sauté onion and celery in drippings until translucent. Stir in garlic and cook for 2 to 3 minutes. Add tomatoes with juice to onion mixture; bring to a simmer, stirring occasionally. Stir in undrained beans; return to a simmer. Add reserved bacon and remaining ingredients except rice to skillet; heat through. To serve, spoon over rice.

Serves 6 to 8

4 to 6 slices bacon, diced
1 onion, diced
1 stalk celery, diced
1 T. garlic, chopped
14-1/2 oz. can diced tomatoes
2 15-1/2 oz. cans cannellini beans
hot pepper sauce and red pepper flakes to taste
1/8 t. Italian seasoning
2 to 3 T. butter
salt and pepper to taste
cooked rice

FRESH BROCCOLI SALAD

DONNA HUNGERFORD
AURORA, CO

*My mom used to make broccoli salad often in the
summertime. Now, whenever I go to a salad bar,
broccoli salad is the first thing I put on my plate to
see if I like the blend of ingredients!*

**2 bunches broccoli,
finely chopped**

**1 c. sharp Cheddar
cheese, shredded or
diced**

1 onion, chopped

**10 slices bacon, crisply
cooked and chopped**

**1/4 to 1/2 c. sunflower
seed kernels**

**3/4 to 1 c. mayonnaise
or mayonnaise-style
salad dressing**

**3 to 4 T. sugar or sugar
substitute**

3 to 4 T. white vinegar

**salt or salt-free
seasoning and pepper
to taste**

In a large bowl, combine broccoli, cheese, onion,
bacon and sunflower seeds. In a small bowl,
combine remaining ingredients. Pour dressing
over broccoli mixture; mix to coat well. Cover and
refrigerate until serving time.

Serves 6 to 10

LOUISE'S POTATO SALAD

DENISE NEAL
CASTLE ROCK, CO

This recipe was handed down in my husband's family. His Portuguese grandma would make this often...it's one of the things they remember best about her cooking.

Keep potatoes warm while preparing other ingredients. Slice one egg and set aside for garnish. Dice remaining eggs; place in a large bowl and add remaining ingredients except garnish. Add potatoes to bowl while still warm; toss gently to coat. Garnish with sliced egg, paprika and parsley. Refrigerate until serving time.

Serves 10

5 lbs. potatoes, peeled, cubed and cooked in salted water

4 eggs, hard-boiled, peeled and divided

1/4 c. mayonnaise

1/2 red onion, chopped

2 stalks celery, chopped

1 T. sweet pickle relish

1/2 t. celery salt

1/2 t. dried parsley

Garnish: paprika, fresh parsley

NO-MAYO CABBAGE SALAD

SANDRA SULLIVAN
AURORA, CO

This salad is awesome for picnics or camping! Make it several days ahead...the longer it's refrigerated, the crisper it gets.

1 head cabbage, shredded
1 onion, chopped
1 green pepper, chopped
1 c. boiling water
1 T. salt
1 c. sugar
1 c. white vinegar
1 T. celery seed
Optional: 1/2 c. carrots, peeled and shredded

In a large bowl, combine cabbage, onion, green pepper, boiling water and salt. Stir well; let stand for hour. Drain and add remaining ingredients; mix well. Cover and refrigerate until serving time. Salad will become crisper as it chills.

Serves 6

PRESNTATION

Cookie cutters make the cutest napkin rings...what fun take-home gifts for guests!

GREEN CHILE MAC & CHEESE

TRISH PATTERSON
COLORADO SPRINGS, CO

This quick and tasty recipe came from a neighbor and it has become a family favorite. The ingredients can be kept in your pantry. Use canned green chiles of the heat level your family can tolerate!

Combine soup and milk in a saucepan over medium-high heat. Stir until smooth; add uncooked macaroni. Bring to a boil; reduce heat to medium. Simmer over medium heat for 10 to 15 minutes, until macaroni is tender, stirring often to avoid burning. Stir in undrained chiles; heat through.

Serves 4

10-3/4 oz. can Cheddar cheese soup
1-1/4 c. milk
1 c. elbow macaroni, uncooked
4-oz. can diced green chiles

BAKED HOMESTYLE FRENCH FRIES

ANNE PTACNIK
YUMA, CO

These hot-from-the-oven fries are a staple in our family. My three young kids love them alongside burgers from the grill. We think they taste just as good as the fried version!

4 russet potatoes, sliced into thin strips

3 to 4 T. oil

garlic powder, salt and pepper to taste

2 T. grated Parmesan cheese

Garnish: catsup or barbecue sauce

Arrange potatoes in a single layer on a baking sheet. Drizzle with oil; sprinkle with seasonings and Parmesan cheese. Toss with hands. Bake at 400 degrees for 20 minutes, or to desired crispness, occasionally turning fries with a spatula for even baking. Serve hot with catsup or barbecue sauce.

Serves 4 to 6

SKILLET MACARONI & CHEESE

MICHELLE TAGGART
PARKER, CO

I first made this recipe back in high school. It's wonderful for summer days when you don't want to heat up the kitchen by turning on the oven.

Melt butter in a skillet over low heat. Add uncooked macaroni, onion, green pepper and seasonings; cook until onion is transparent. Add water; stir and bring to a boil. Cover and simmer for 20 minutes, or until tender. Sprinkle flour over macaroni mixture and blend in; stir in cheese and evaporated milk. Continue to simmer for 5 minutes at low temperature, or until cheese melts.

Serves 4 to 6

1/2 c. butter

2 c. elbow macaroni, uncooked and divided

1/2 c. onion, chopped

1/2 c. green pepper, chopped

1-1/4 t. salt

1/4 t. pepper

1/4 t. dry mustard

2 c. water

1 T. all-purpose flour

8-oz. pkg. shredded Cheddar cheese

12-oz. can evaporated milk

CRANBERRY-JALAPEÑO RELISH

SHONA MACAN
LOVELAND, CO

I found this recipe in an old newspaper clipping...a tasty change from traditional cranberry relish. Remember to make a day ahead to allow the flavors to blend.

1 c. sugar
1 c. water
12-oz. pkg. cranberries
2 jalapeños, seeded and minced
1 T. fresh cilantro, chopped
1/2 t. ground cumin
2 to 3 green onions, sliced
1 T. lime juice

Combine sugar and water in a saucepan over medium heat; bring to a boil. Add cranberries; return to a boil. Cook for 10 minutes without stirring. Pour into a bowl and allow to cool. Add remaining ingredients; mix gently. Refrigerate. Serve chilled or at room temperature.

Serves 8

CARAMELIZED BRUSSELS SPROUTS

BETH SCHLIEPER
LAKEWOOD, CO

*These go great with a golden turkey and all the trimmings. My friend
Lisa and I usually eat any leftovers before we can put them away!*

Steam Brussels sprouts for 8 to 10 minutes, or until just tender-crisp. Melt butter in a deep skillet. Add onions and 3 tablespoons vinegar; cook until golden. Add Brussels sprouts, sugar and remaining vinegar. Sauté over medium heat until sprouts are lightly caramelized. Sprinkle with salt, pepper and nuts, if desired.

Serves 8

4 lbs. Brussels sprouts, trimmed
1/2 c. butter
4 onions, cut into strips
1/4 c. red wine vinegar, divided
2 T. sugar
salt and pepper to taste
Optional: 1/2 c. pistachio nuts, chopped

HONEY-GINGER CARROTS

DENISE NEAL
CASTLE ROCK, CO

This is our favorite way to eat cooked carrots...my kids love it! This stovetop version is quick to fix. I like to speed it up even more by buying the carrots already waffle-cut into slices.

1 lb. carrots, peeled and sliced

1/4 t. salt

1/4 c. butter

3 T. honey

1 to 1-1/2 t. fresh ginger, peeled and grated

Garnish: chopped fresh parsley

Place carrots in a saucepan; add a small amount of water to just cover carrots. Sprinkle with salt. Cook over medium-high heat just until carrots are tender; drain. Remove from heat. Add butter, honey and ginger; stir until butter and honey are melted. Garnish with chopped parsley.

Serves 4

MACK'S HONEY APPLE RINGS

VICKIE RODDIE
EVERGREEN, CO

A scrumptious garnish for pork chops or sausage.

Combine honey, vinegar, cinnamon and salt in a large skillet; bring to a boil over medium heat. Add apple rings to skillet. Reduce heat and simmer for 8 to 10 minutes until tender, turning apples once.

Serves 4

1/2 c. honey

2 T. vinegar

1/4 t. cinnamon

1/4 t. salt

4 Golden Delicious apples, cored and cut into 1/2-inch rings

MOM'S HOMINY & CHEESE

LINDA WALKER
ERIE, CO

This old-fashioned recipe came from my mother, who is no longer with us. She got it from the ladies of the Methodist church in Arvada, Colorado, where she worked for 25 years. I always think of her, and them when I make it. It is especially tasty with BBQ beef.

- 3 T. butter
- 1/4 c. onion, finely chopped
- 3 T. all-purpose flour
- 3/4 t. chili powder
- 1 t. salt
- 1/8 t. pepper
- 1-1/2 c. milk
- 2 15-oz. cans white hominy, drained and rinsed
- 8-oz. pkg. shredded Cheddar cheese

In a large saucepan over medium heat, melt butter and sauté onion until tender. Add flour and seasonings; cook and stir until bubbly. Slowly add milk; cook and stir until thickened. Stir in hominy; turn into a buttered 1-1/2 quart casserole dish. Top with cheese. Bake, uncovered, at 350 degrees for 35 to 40 minutes.

Serves 6

LUCY'S SAUSAGE SALAD

LUCY DAVIS
COLORADO SPRINGS, CO

This deliciously different salad may be made ahead and chilled for one to two hours, or served immediately.

Measure out half the sausages; set aside for a future use. Slice remaining sausages into 3 pieces each. In a skillet, sauté sausages in oil over medium heat until lightly golden; drain. In a large bowl, combine corn, beans, jalapeño and red pepper. Stir in sausage. Toss with Dressing; garnish with cilantro.

Dressing: Whisk together all ingredients.

Serves 4

14-oz. pkg. mini smoked beef sausages, divided

1 t. canola oil

1 c. corn

15-1/2 oz. can black beans, drained and rinsed

1 T. canned jalapeño pepper, seeded and minced

1 c. red pepper, chopped

Garnish: fresh cilantro sprigs

DRESSING

3 T. low-fat plain yogurt

3 T. low-fat sour cream

1/4 c. picante sauce

1/2 c. fresh cilantro, chopped

salt and pepper to taste

WHITE BEAN & TOMATO SALAD

DENISE NEAL
CASTLE ROCK, CO

I got this delicious recipe while on vacation in England. We love it! If you can't get cannellini beans, navy beans will work fine.

- **15-oz. can cannellini beans, drained and rinsed**
- **2 zucchini or yellow squash, diced**
- **1 pt. cherry tomatoes, halved**
- **1/2 c. red onion, chopped**
- **3 T. olive oil**
- **2 T. lemon juice**
- **1/4 c. fresh cilantro, chopped**

Combine all ingredients in a large bowl. Cover and refrigerate. Let stand at room temperature 20 to 30 minutes before serving.

Serves 6

CELERY SEED SLAW

SANDRA SULLIVAN
AURORA, CO

A simple cooked dressing gives crisp cabbage a delightful break from mayonnaise-based coleslaw. It's perfect for potlucks.

Combine cabbage, carrot and green pepper in a heatproof bowl; set aside. In a saucepan over medium heat, combine vinegar, sugar, salt and celery seed. Bring to a boil; stir until sugar dissolves. Pour hot vinegar mixture over cabbage mixture; toss well. Cover and refrigerate for 4 hours to overnight. Toss again before serving.

Serves 12

3 lbs. cabbage, chopped
1/2 c. carrot, peeled and shredded
1/2 c. green pepper, chopped
1 c. cider vinegar
1 c. sugar
1 T. salt
1 t. celery seed

JUST FOR FUN

The highest suspension bridge in the world is over the Royal Gorge. The Royal Gorge Bridge spans the Arkansas River at a height of 1,053 feet.

GARDEN-FRESH SPICY TOMATO SALAD

LINDA BROWN
LONE TREE, CO

Just the recipe to make when you have too many fresh tomatoes or simply want a different salad for a change. Cool and refreshing with a lively kick!

3 tomatoes, chopped
1/2 c. red onion, chopped
1 cucumber, chopped
1 T. red pepper flakes
1/4 c. rice wine vinegar

Place vegetables in a glass serving bowl. Add pepper flakes and vinegar; toss to mix well. Cover and chill. Stir just before serving.

Serves 4

CHEESY MASHED POTATO PANCAKES

ANNE PTACNIK
YUMA, CO

A tasty way to use up leftover mashed potatoes. Fry them in a heavy cast-iron skillet to create crispy, cheesy edges that everyone will love!

3 c. mashed potatoes
3/4 c. shredded Cheddar cheese
salt and pepper to taste
1/4 c. butter, divided

In a bowl, combine all ingredients except butter. Form into pancake-like patties, using 1/3 to 1/2 cup potato mixture for each. In a skillet over medium heat, melt 1/2 to one tablespoon butter. Add several patties to skillet. Cook until crisp and golden; turn to cook other side. Add more butter to skillet for each batch. Serve warm.

Serves 6 to 8

CLASSIC COBB SALAD

JO ANN
GOOSEBERRY PATCH

So pretty on a luncheon buffet...just add a basket of fruit muffins and a pitcher of ice tea.

Cover a large serving platter with lettuce. Arrange remaining ingredients in rows over lettuce, one ingredient at a time. Drizzle with Red Wine Dressing just before serving.

Red Wine Dressing: In a jar with a tight-fitting lid, combine all ingredients except olive oil and garlic. Cover jar and shake well. Add oil and garlic; cover and shake again. Shake again just before serving.

Serves 6 to 8

1 head iceberg lettuce, chopped
1 c. cooked chicken breast, cubed
1 c. cooked ham, cubed
8 slices bacon, crisply cooked and crumbled
3 to 4 eggs, hard-boiled, peeled and sliced
1 to 2 tomatoes, cubed
1 avocado, halved, pitted and cubed
1/2 c. crumbled blue cheese
1/2 c. fresh parsley, chopped

RED WINE DRESSING
1/4 c. red wine vinegar
3/4 t. salt
1/2 t. dry mustard
1/8 t. pepper
1/2 c. olive oil
1 clove garlic, pressed

SURPRISE SCALLOPED CORN

JANA TEMPLE
COLORADO SPRINGS, CO

This is my mother's recipe that has been handed down to me and now to my grown daughters. It is very special to us. She passed away some time ago, and I am happy to share it in her honor.

14-3/4 oz. can cream-style corn

15-oz. can corn, drained

1/4 c. butter, melted and slightly cooled

8-1/2 oz. pkg. corn muffin mix

2 eggs, beaten

1/4 c. sugar

8-oz. container sour cream

1 c. shredded Cheddar cheese

In a large bowl, mix together all ingredients. Spoon into a greased 3-quart casserole dish. Batter will rise slightly during baking, so make sure there is 1/2 to one-inch space in dish above batter. Bake, uncovered, at 350 degrees for 50 to 60 minutes, until golden.

Serves 4 to 6

ROASTED BASIL TOMATOES

DENISE NEAL
CASTLE ROCK, CO

*Leftovers are so good served over cooked pasta. Use a potato peeler
to get nice slivers of fresh Parmesan cheese.*

Heat oil in a saucepan over medium heat. Place
tomato halves cut-side down in saucepan. Cook
5 to 8 minutes. Arrange tomatoes, cut-side up, in a
lightly greased 8"x8" baking pan. Pour any liquid in
saucepan over tomatoes. Sprinkle with basil and salt.
Bake, uncovered, at 400 degrees for 20 to
30 minutes. Garnish with cheese.

Serves 4 to 6

1/3 c. olive oil

8 to 10 roma tomatoes,
  halved lengthwise

1 to 2 t. dried basil or
  1 to 2 T. fresh basil,
  chopped, to taste

salt to taste

Garnish: Parmesan
  cheese slivers

CHAPTER THREE

Saddle-Up

Sandwiches, Soups & Breads

GATHER 'ROUND THE CAMPFIRE

TOGETHER WITH FAMILY & FRIENDS

TO COZY UP WITH A BOWL OF

HEARTY SOUP OR A TASTY

SANDWICH PERFECT FOR PACK'N IN

THE SADDLE BAG!

CHEESY WHITE CHICKEN CHILI

HOLLY CHILD
PARKER, CO

I love to bring out this chili recipe when the weather starts getting chillier. It's so hearty and will warm you up on the coldest nights.

4 to 6 boneless, skinless chicken breasts, cooked and cubed

6 c. chicken broth

4 16-oz. cans Great Northern beans, drained and rinsed

4-oz. can green chiles

1 onion, chopped

1 T. garlic, minced

1 T. ground cumin

1-1/2 t. dried oregano

1-1/2 c. shredded Monterey Jack cheese

Combine all ingredients except cheese in a large slow cooker. Cover and cook on high setting for 4 to 6 hours. During the last hour, turn slow cooker to low setting. Stir in cheese; let stand for several minutes, until cheese is completely melted.

Serves 8

SANTA FE CHICKEN SOUP

BARB GRIFFITH
FORT COLLINS, CO

Every Christmas Eve, when our family returns from church services we look forward to sitting down to our traditional soup supper.

In a microwave-safe bowl, combine cheese and tomatoes with chiles. Cover and microwave on high setting for 5 minutes. Meanwhile, combine remaining ingredients, except chips or crackers, in a large slow cooker. Stir cheese mixture; spoon into slow cooker. Cover and cook on high setting for 2 to 3 hours. Serve with corn chips or crackers.

Serves 8 to 10

16-oz. pkg. pasteurized process cheese spread, cubed

10-oz. can diced tomatoes with green chiles

1 lb. boneless, skinless chicken, cooked and cubed

15-1/2 oz. can pinto beans, drained and rinsed

14-1/2 oz. can stewed tomatoes

15-1/4 oz. can corn, drained

1 onion, chopped

corn chips or crackers

VEGETABLE CHILI

MICHELLE TAGGART
PARKER, CO

I created this recipe one day when I was trying to make chili healthier for my family. It's chock-full of veggies!

1 lb. ground beef, browned and drained

2 14-1/2 oz. cans diced tomatoes

1 onion, diced

2 zucchini, diced

3 carrots, peeled and diced

2 15-oz. cans black-eyed peas, drained and rinsed

15-oz. can pinto beans, drained and rinsed

15-1/4 oz. can corn, drained

1-1/4 oz. pkg. chili seasoning mix

Garnish: shredded Cheddar cheese

Add beef, tomatoes with juice and remaining ingredients except cheese to a slow cooker; mix well. Cover and cook on low setting for 3 to 4 hours. To serve, ladle into bowls and sprinkle with cheese.

Serves 8 to 10

MOM'S OXTAIL SOUP

BOBBIE KEEFER
BYERS, CO

Soups were an important part of my German mom's recipe collection. Cabbage was often used in her delicious soups. Oxtail Soup, or Ochsenschwanzsuppe, is a favorite family heirloom recipe.

Season oxtails with salt and pepper; set aside. Heat butter and oil in a large skillet over medium-high heat. Brown oxtails on all sides; remove to a slow cooker, reserving drippings in skillet. Add onion and garlic to reserved drippings. Cook for 5 to 10 minutes, stirring often, until caramelized. Add broth to skillet; simmer for a few minutes, stirring up any browned bits in bottom of skillet. Add skillet mixture to slow cooker along with undrained tomatoes and remaining ingredients. Cover and cook on high setting for 8 hours, or until vegetables are tender and meat pulls easily away from the bones. Discard bones before serving.

Serves 8

2 lbs. beef oxtails
salt and pepper to taste
1 T. butter
1 T. oil
1 onion, chopped
2 cloves garlic, minced
14-1/2 oz. can beef broth
2 14-1/2 oz. cans diced
  tomatoes
1 head cabbage, chopped
3 carrots, peeled and
  diced
2 t. dried parsley
1 t. dried thyme
1 t. bay leaves, crumbled

PASTA FAGIOLI SOUP

MARLA KINNERSLEY
LITTLETON, CO

This is one of my favorite go-to soups! I make it a lot for Sunday dinners and then we have leftovers for busy Mondays. It is very satisfying served with bread sticks and a crisp tossed salad.

1 lb. ground beef

1 yellow onion, chopped

14-1/2 oz. can diced tomatoes

26-oz. jar spaghetti sauce

2 14-1/2 oz. cans beef broth

15-1/2 oz. can kidney beans, drained and rinsed

1 c. carrots, peeled and grated

1 c. celery, sliced

1 T. white balsamic vinegar

1 t. dried basil

1 t. dried oregano

1/2 t. dried thyme

1/2 t. pepper

1/2 t. hot pepper sauce

1-1/2 c. small shell pasta, uncooked

2 t. fresh parsley, chopped

In a skillet over medium heat, brown beef with onion. Drain; add beef mixture to a 5-quart slow cooker. Add tomatoes with juice and remaining ingredients except pasta and parsley; stir. Cover and cook on low setting for 7 to 8 hours. About 15 minutes before serving, stir in pasta and parsley. Cover and cook on low setting for 15 minutes more, or until pasta is tender.

Serves 8

MOM'S KIELBASA STEW

HOLLI PURKEYPILE
HOLYOKE, CO

Years ago, my mom and I were putting together a family cookbook. Sadly, she passed away and we never finished it. When my family moved, I found the unfinished project in a dust-covered box under the bed. I finished the cookbook and had it printed in her memory. I am so glad that I did, because I have found some of the best "forgotten" recipes in it, including this one!

1/2 lb. cabbage, chopped

In a stockpot over medium heat, brown sausage. Drain; remove sausage and set aside. To the same pot, add one cup broth, onion and garlic. Bring to a boil over high heat; simmer until onion is tender. Stir in remaining broth, beans and cabbage; return sausage to pan. Reduce heat to medium-low; cover and simmer for 20 to 30 minutes, until cabbage is tender.

Serves 6

1 lb. Polish sausage, sliced 1/2-inch thick

3 c. chicken broth, divided

1 c. onion, chopped

1 T. garlic, minced

2 16-oz. cans navy beans

CHICKEN POT PIE SOUP

CARRIE ALLEN
DILLON, CO

This soup smells and tastes like fall to me! I love to make it on cool days to warm up my family. You can also thicken the soup a little more and top with a crust for a delicious chicken pot pie.

2 c. potatoes, peeled and cubed

1 c. carrots, peeled and sliced

1 c. frozen petite green peas

6 T. butter, sliced

1/3 c. all-purpose flour

4 c. whole milk

5 t. chicken bouillon granules

1/4 t. pepper

2 c. cooked chicken, cubed

In a soup pot, cover potatoes and carrots with water. Cook over medium-high heat until tender, 10 to 15 minutes. Add peas; cook until tender, 3 to 5 minutes. Drain; set vegetables aside in a bowl. In the same pot, melt butter over medium heat. Stir in flour; cook and stir until mixture is golden. Add milk, bouillon and pepper to butter mixture. Cook and stir over medium heat until thickened. Add chicken and vegetables; heat through.

Serves 5 to 6

FREEZER ONION SOUP

SANDRA SULLIVAN
AURORA, CO

I use my home-grown onions in this recipe. We take jars of this soup to ski buddies over the holidays. It tastes so good after a day on the slopes...who wouldn't love to receive a jar of savory soup?

In a heavy saucepan over medium heat, cook onions in butter until transparent and golden. Add sugar and mustard. Blend in flour; gradually stir in beef broth and sherry or broth. Simmer for 30 minutes. Season with salt and pepper. Cool; ladle into freezer-safe containers, leaving 1/2-inch headspace. Seal containers and freeze for up to 2 months. Thaw and reheat to serve. If desired, ladle into individual oven-proof bowls; top with croutons and cheese. Broil for 2 to 3 minutes, until cheese is melted.

Serves 8

2 lbs. onions, sliced
6 T. butter
1 t. sugar
1 t. dry mustard
3 T. all-purpose flour
8 c. beef broth
1 c. dry sherry or beef broth
salt and pepper to taste
Optional: croutons, shredded Swiss cheese

KITCHEN TIP

A 250-degree oven keeps hot appetizers toasty until you're ready to serve them.

CARNITAS SOUP

**DONNA LANDWEHR
WHEAT RIDGE, CO**

This soup was made in a pinch for dinner one night, using items on hand. It's a very warming and hearty soup. It's also easy to double or triple the recipe and freeze the extra. The heat level can easily be changed up by mixing mild and spicy tomatoes.

2 10-oz. cans diced tomatoes with green chiles
15-oz. can black beans, drained and rinsed
2 14-oz. cans chicken broth
16-oz. pkg. pre-cooked pork carnitas, diced

Combine all ingredients in a soup pot over medium heat, adding desired amount of carnitas. Amount of broth may be adjusted to desired consistency. Cook until heated through, stirring occasionally, about 30 minutes.

Serves 4

SOUTHWESTERN FLATBREAD

**RITA MORGAN
PUEBLO, CO**

Yum...hot fresh-baked bread to enjoy with your soup! Easy to change up to Italian flavors too, with oregano and Parmesan cheese.

2 t. olive oil, divided
11-oz. tube refrigerated crusty French loaf
1/2 c. roasted sunflower kernels
1 t. chili powder
1/2 to 1 t. coarse salt

Brush a 15"x10" jelly-roll pan with one teaspoon oil; unroll dough onto pan. Use a floured rolling pin to roll out into a rectangle. Drizzle dough with remaining oil; brush over dough. In a small bowl, combine sunflower kernels and chili powder; mix well and sprinkle over dough. Firmly press kernels into dough; sprinkle with salt. Bake at 375 degrees for 12 to 16 minutes, until golden. Remove flatbread to a wire rack; cool 10 minutes. Tear or cut into pieces.

Makes 15 pieces

END-OF-THE-GARDEN SOUP

SANDRA SULLIVAN
AURORA, CO

So delicious on a cold day! Tuck this soup in your freezer... a great way to capture fresh summer flavors. Add other favorite vegetables, if you like.

Combine all ingredients in a large soup pot. Bring to a boil over medium heat; reduce heat to low. Cover and simmer for one hour, stirring occasionally. Season with additional salt and pepper, as desired. Ladle soup into one-quart containers; attach serving directions and freeze.

To serve: For each thawed one-quart container of soup, brown 1/2 pound ground beef or Italian ground pork sausage; drain. Add soup; bring to a boil. Simmer over low heat for 15 to 20 minutes. Season with additional salt and pepper, as needed.

Makes 8 quarts, 4 servings per quart

16 c. tomatoes, diced
2 c. green beans, sliced
2 c. yellow beans, sliced
2 c. carrots, peeled and sliced
1 head cabbage, chopped
1/2 bunch celery, chopped
1 green pepper, chopped
1 onion, chopped
3 c. beef or vegetable broth
3 c. tomato juice
salt and pepper to taste

HERB BREAD

CARA LORENZ
OLATHE, CO

My sister-in-law shared this delicious recipe with me. It is very easy to stir up and makes the kitchen smell so good while it's baking.

1 env. active dry yeast
1-3/4 c. warm water
4 c. all-purpose flour
3 T. sugar
1 t. salt
1 t. garlic salt
1/2 t. dried oregano
1/2 t. dried basil
1/2 t. dried parsley
Garnish: melted butter

Add yeast to warm water, 110 to 115 degrees; stir to dissolve. Blend in remaining ingredients except butter; stir until smooth. Cover with a tea towel; set aside until double in bulk. Punch down and turn dough out on a lightly floured surface. Knead until smooth and bubbles have disappeared. Divide dough in half and shape into 2 loaves. Place in 2 greased 9"x5" loaf pans; cover and let rise again until double. Bake at 350 degrees for 35 to 40 minutes. Remove from pans and brush with butter. While bread is still warm, place in plastic zipping bags to keep moist.

Makes 2 loaves

SAVORY CHEESE BISCUITS

J. C. SCHMELTEKOPF
JOHNSTOWN, CO

I've been making biscuits for almost 50 years, since I was ten years old. I have always loved my cheese biscuits best...they go great with soups, stews and beans. They are addictive!

2 c. biscuit baking mix
1/2 c. shredded Cheddar cheese
1-1/2 t. dried parsley
1/8 t. garlic salt
2/3 c. milk
1/4 c. butter, melted
1/4 t. garlic powder

In a bowl, combine biscuit mix, cheese, parsley and garlic salt. Stir in milk until a soft dough forms. Pat out dough on a floured surface; cut out 8 biscuits with a round cutter. Press each biscuit into a muffin cup coated with non-stick vegetable spray. Bake at 425 degrees for 10 to 15 minutes, until golden. Mix butter and garlic powder in a small bowl; brush over biscuits. Serve warm.

Makes 8 biscuits

SUMMER SQUASH CHOWDER

CHERYL DONNELLY
ARVADA, CO

I love this soup in the late summer and early fall when the garden and farmers' markets are bursting with fresh produce. If it's made off-season, frozen corn is a good substitute…just reduce the cooking time to 2 minutes once it's added.

In a soup pot over medium heat, cook bacon until crisp. Set aside bacon and drain, reserving drippings in soup pot. Add onion, garlic and yellow or red pepper into soup pot; sauté 5 minutes. Sprinkle flour evenly over vegetables and cook one minute. Add 1/2 cup broth, stirring well to blend. Cook over medium heat until thickened. Pour in remaining broth, milk, zucchini, squash, sauces, thyme and salt. Bring to a boil. Reduce heat and simmer, covered, 15 minutes, stirring occasionally. Add corn to a saucepan; cover with water. Cook over medium heat 5 minutes. Drain and stir into soup mixture. Add reserved bacon, juice and parsley. Heat through and add pepper to taste.

4 slices bacon, chopped
1 onion, finely diced
1 clove garlic, minced
1 yellow or red pepper, finely diced
2 T. all-purpose flour
14-1/2 oz. can vegetable broth, divided
5-oz. can evaporated milk
4 zucchini, diced
2 yellow squash, diced
1 t. white wine Worcestershire sauce
1/2 t. hot pepper sauce
3/4 t. dried thyme
1/2 t. salt
1 c. fresh corn kernels
2 T. lemon juice
1/2 c. fresh parsley, finely chopped
pepper to taste

GOLDEN SOPAPILLAS

KAY SMITH
LAJARA, CO

Everyone loves these delicious little pillows of hot bread! Serve them with honey butter or stuff with your favorite taco filling.

1-3/4 c. all-purpose flour
2 t. baking powder
1 t. salt
2 T. shortening
2/3 c. cold water
oil for deep frying

In a bowl, mix flour, baking powder and salt. Cut in shortening with a pastry cutter until mixture resembles cornmeal. Stir in water, one tablespoon at a time, until a stiff dough forms; set aside. Add 4 inches of oil to a deep fryer; heat to about 400 degrees. While oil heats, roll out dough on a floured surface until very thin. Cut into 4-inch squares. Test oil by dropping in a small piece of dough; if dough browns quickly, it's ready. Fry each piece until it puffs up; turn over carefully and fry until other side is golden. Lift out with a slotted spoon; drain on paper towels. Serve warm.

Makes one dozen

GREEN CHILE SOUP

BERNADETTE TORRES
MONTE VISTA, CO

I have many fond memories of winter nights, savoring this slow-cooker soup with fresh-baked biscuits or cornbread.

1 lb. ground beef
1/2 c. onion, chopped
1 clove garlic, chopped
5 russet potatoes, peeled and diced
1/2 c. chopped green chiles
1.35-oz. pkg. onion soup mix
6 to 8 c. water, divided
salt and pepper to taste

Brown beef, onion and garlic in a skillet over medium heat; drain. In a slow cooker, combine potatoes, chiles, soup mix and 6 cups water; stir in beef mixture. Add remaining water to cover ingredients as necessary. Cover and cook on low setting for 5 hours. Add salt and pepper to taste.

Serves 4

ORIENTAL CHICKEN SOUP

SANDRA SULLIVAN
AURORA, CO

We enjoy this quick chicken soup on busy weekday evenings. The whole process takes just 20 minutes for homemade soup, and it's yummy and healthy!

In a large soup pot over high heat, bring broth, water, ginger, garlic and red pepper flakes to a boil. Add half of the spaghetti, reserving remainder for a future use. Reduce heat; simmer until spaghetti is tender, about 6 to 8 minutes. Add chicken, pepper and snow peas; simmer until chicken is fully cooked, about 3 minutes. Stir in lime juice, green onions and salt.

Serves 4

3 14-1/2 oz. cans chicken broth

2 c. water

1 T. fresh ginger, peeled and grated

1 clove garlic, slivered

1/4 to 1/2 t. red pepper flakes

8-oz. pkg. whole-wheat spaghetti, uncooked and divided

2 boneless, skinless chicken breasts, thinly sliced

1 red pepper, thinly sliced

1 c. snow peas, chopped

juice of 1 lime

2 green onions, thinly sliced

salt to taste

EASY BROWN BREAD

**TIFFANY BRINKLEY,
BROOMFIELD, CO**

Serve hot and top with lots of butter!

2 c. whole-wheat flour
1 c. all-purpose flour
1 T. baking powder
1 t. salt
2 T. molasses
2 T. oil
1-1/3 c. water

Combine flours, baking powder and salt in a large bowl; stir to mix. Add molasses, oil and water; mix until moistened. Place batter in a greased 5-quart slow cooker. Place 5 paper towels across top of slow cooker to catch any condensation. Cover, placing a wooden toothpick between paper towels and lid to allow steam to escape. Cook on high setting 2 hours; do not uncover while cooking. Loosen sides of bread with a knife; remove from slow cooker and place on a wire rack.

Makes one loaf

CHEESE FRENCHIES

**BRENDA SCHLOSSER
BRIGHTON, CO**

Back in the 60s and 70s, a restaurant chain called King's Food Host served these delicious crunchy-gooey sandwiches. The restaurants are no longer around, but these are just as good, if not better! Perfect comfort food on a cold day with a hot bowl of tomato soup.

6 slices white bread
3 T. mayonnaise
6 slices American cheese
1 egg
1/2 c. milk
3/4 c. all-purpose flour
1 t. salt
1 c. corn flake cereal, crushed
oil for deep frying

Spread bread slices with mayonnaise on one side. Add 2 slices cheese to each of 3 slices; close sandwiches with remaining bread. Cut sandwiches into triangles; trim off crusts, if desired. Whisk together egg, milk, flour and salt in a shallow dish; place crushed cereal in a separate dish. Dip each triangle into egg mixture; coat with cereal. Add one inch oil to a skillet over medium-high heat; heat to 375 degrees. Add triangles; deep-fry until golden on both sides. Place on paper towels to drain.

Serves 3

GRILLED GOUDA SANDWICHES

TIFFANY BRINKLEY
BROOMFIELD, CO

Good ol' grilled cheese, all grown up.

Rub one side of each slice of bread with garlic. Place 4 bread slices garlic-side down; top each bread slice with one teaspoon mustard and 2 slices Gouda. Place remaining bread slices, garlic-side up, on sandwich bottoms. Combine butter, cayenne pepper and pepper in a small bowl; brush mixture over each side of sandwiches. Cook sandwiches in an oven-proof skillet over medium-high heat for about 2 minutes on each side, until golden. Place skillet in oven and bake at 400 degrees for about 5 minutes, until cheese is melted. Slice sandwiches diagonally.

Makes 4 sandwiches

8 slices country-style bread

1 clove garlic, halved

4 t. Dijon mustard

1/2 lb. sliced Gouda cheese

2 T. butter, melted

1/8 t. cayenne pepper

1/8 t. pepper

NEW YEAR'S BLACK–EYED PEA STEW

SHANNON SWINDALL
LITTLETON, CO

I put this stew together after I heard it was lucky to eat black-eyed peas on New Year's Day. I use leftover Christmas ham or turkey. Serve with salad, rolls and sparkling juice to toast in the New Year.

Layer ham or turkey, broth, tomatoes with juice, peas and onion in a 4-quart slow cooker. Cover and cook on high setting for 5 to 6 hours; stir occasionally

Makes 6 servings

2 c. cooked ham or turkey, chopped

14-oz. can chicken or beef broth

14-1/2 oz. can Italian-style diced tomatoes

12-oz. pkg. frozen black-eyed peas, or 2 15-oz. cans black-eyed peas

1 onion, chopped

NORTH WOODS BEAN SOUP

**SHARON DEMERS
DOLORES, CO**

Here is a great soup to come home to on a brisk, cool evening.

1/2 lb. turkey Kielbasa, halved lengthwise and sliced
1/2-inch thick
1 c. baby carrots, chopped
1 c. onion, chopped
2 cloves garlic, minced
4 c. chicken broth
1/2 t. Italian seasoning
1/2 t. pepper
2 15.8-oz. cans Great Northern beans, drained and rinsed
6-oz. pkg. baby spinach

Spray a large stockpot with non-stick vegetable spray; heat over medium-high heat. Add Kielbasa, carrots, onion and garlic; sauté for 3 minutes, stirring occasionally. Reduce heat to medium; cook for 5 minutes. Add broth, seasonings and beans. Bring to a boil; reduce heat and simmer for 5 minutes. Place 2 cups of soup in a blender or food processor. Process until smooth; return processed soup to pan. Simmer for an additional 5 minutes; remove from heat. Add spinach, stirring until it wilts.

Serves 5

COLORADO FUN FACT

Denver lays claim to the invention of the cheeseburger. The trademark for the name Cheeseburger was awarded on March 5, 1935 to Louis Ballast. His Humpty Dumpty restaurant at 2776 North Speer Blvd. is now a Key Bank.

ZUCCHINI–TORTELLINI HARVEST SOUP

KATHI NOLAND
LAKEWOOD, CO

I love this slow-cooker soup recipe made with the vegetables I harvest from my garden in late summer. Serve with buttered crusty French rolls.

In a slow cooker, combine all ingredients except zucchini, tortellini and garnish. Cover and cook on low setting for 5 to 7 hours. Add zucchini and tortellini to slow cooker; cover and cook on low setting for one additional hour. At serving time, discard bay leaf. Ladle into soup bowls; garnish with curls of Parmesan cheese.

Serves 6

1 lb. Italian pork sausage links, browned and thinly sliced

1 onion, chopped

1 to 2 carrots, peeled and chopped

2 c. tomatoes, diced

2 14-oz. cans vegetable broth

14-oz. can pizza sauce

2 c. water

1 bay leaf

1 to 2 zucchini, shredded or sliced

9-oz. pkg. refrigerated cheese tortellini, uncooked

Garnish: Parmesan cheese curls

RED DEVIL FRANKS

SARA WRIGHT
COLORADO SPRINGS, CO

*My grandmother used to make these tasty franks for her
father in the 1940s. The sauce just can't be beat...it has such
a unique and delicious flavor!*

2 to 4 T. butter
1 c. onion, finely chopped
2 cloves garlic, chopped
1-1/2 T. Worcestershire
  sauce
1-1/2 T. mustard
1-1/2 t. sugar
1/2 t. salt
1/8 t. pepper
1/2 c. chili sauce
1 lb. hot dogs
hot dog buns, split

Melt butter in a skillet over medium heat. Cook
onion and garlic in butter until translucent. Add
remaining ingredients except hot dogs and buns to
onion mixture; stir. Cook, stirring occasionally, until
heated through, about 5 minutes. Split hot dogs
lengthwise and arrange in a single layer in a broiler
pan. Spoon sauce over hot dogs; broil until bubbly,
about 5 minutes. Serve hot dogs on buns, topped
with sauce.

Serves 8

AVOCADO EGG SALAD

CRYSTAL BRUNS
ILIFF, CO

*A fresh and delicious twist on egg salad...serve it on your favorite
hearty bread!*

6 eggs, hard-boiled,
  peeled and chopped
2 avocados, pitted, peeled
  and cubed
1/2 c. red onion, minced
3 T. sweet pickles,
  chopped
1 T. mustard
1/3 c. mayonnaise
salt and pepper to taste

Mash eggs with a fork in a bowl until crumbly. Add
remaining ingredients except salt and pepper. Gently
mix ingredients together until blended. Add salt and
pepper to taste.

Serves 6

MIMI'S CORN CHOWDER

RACHEL HILL
CENTER, TX

My daughter "adopted" a very special lady in our church, our pastor's wife. She started calling her MiMi, and since she makes the most wonderful corn chowder, this is how it got its name!

Mix all ingredients together in a slow cooker. Cover and cook on low setting for 3 to 4 hours, until potatoes are tender.

Serves 4 to 6

3 slices bacon, crisply cooked and crumbled

1/4 c. onion, chopped

2 c. creamed corn

1 c. chicken broth

1 pt. light cream

6 saltine crackers, crushed

1 c. shredded Cheddar cheese

16-oz. pkg. frozen diced potatoes

salt and pepper to taste

TEXAS TORTILLA SOUP

JACKIE ANTWEILER
EVERGREEN, CO

Just open 4 cans, heat and eat...how easy is that? Often I'll make it heartier by adding leftovers from the fridge like cooked chicken, leftover rice, fresh tomatoes, garbanzos or red beans. We like it just the way it is, though!

Combine soup and undrained vegetables in a large saucepan. Cook over medium heat until heated through. Ladle into soup bowls; top with cheese and tortilla chips.

Serves 4

26-oz. can chicken and rice soup

10-oz. can diced tomatoes with green chiles

15-oz. can black beans

11-oz. can corn

Garnish: shredded Cheddar cheese, crushed tortilla chips

KIELBASA CHOWDER

JASMINE CLIFTON
COLORADO SPRINGS, CO

I've been making this soup for several years and, without a doubt, it's my most-requested recipe. Everyone raves about it...try it and see if you don't agree!

1/4 c. butter

2 sweet onions, thinly sliced

salt and pepper to taste

1/8 t. allspice

2 potatoes, peeled and diced

3 c. chicken broth

1 qt. half-and-half

14-oz. pkg. frozen corn

14-oz. pkg. Kielbasa sausage, cut into bite-size pieces

Melt butter in a stockpot over medium-high heat. Stir in onions; sprinkle with seasonings. Cook until dark and caramelized, about 8 minutes, stirring frequently. Add potatoes and broth. Reduce heat; simmer until potatoes are tender, about 15 minutes. Add half-and-half and corn; heat through. Remove 3 cups soup to a blender; process on high setting and return to stockpot. Add sausage; heat through. Season with additional salt and pepper as needed.

Serves 6 to 8

BOUILLABAISSE GUMBO

MYRNA SALMON
MONTROSE, CO

I've had this delicious recipe for over thirty years. If you like seafood, you'll love this! Serve with French bread or cornbread.

In a large pot, combine all ingredients except shrimp, clams, oregano, salt and pepper. Cover and simmer over medium-low heat for 30 minutes, or until vegetables are tender. Add shrimp and undrained clams; simmer 10 minutes. Stir in remaining ingredients. Remove bay leaf before serving.

Serves 6 to 8

16-oz. can stewed tomatoes with jalapeños

10-3/4 oz. can tomato soup

10-3/4 oz. can chicken gumbo soup

3 c. water

1 c. sweet potato, peeled and chopped

1/4 c. celery, chopped

1/4 c. carrots, peeled and chopped

1/3 c. green onions, chopped

1 T. fresh parsley, chopped

1 T. fresh cilantro, chopped

1 T. Worcestershire sauce

1 clove garlic, minced

1 bay leaf

1/2 lb. uncooked medium shrimp, cleaned

8-oz. can minced clams

1/4 to 1/2 t. dried oregano

salt and pepper to taste

HEARTY HOMINY BEEF STEW

RITA MORGAN
PUEBLO, CO

We like to top our soup with some sliced avocado for extra flavor and a little more creaminess.

1 onion, chopped

2-lb. beef chuck roast, cubed

1/4 t. salt

1 green pepper, chopped

3 carrots, peeled and sliced

3 stalks celery, sliced

3 cloves garlic, minced

14-1/2 oz. can petite diced tomatoes

1 c. beef broth, divided

2 T. cornstarch

15-oz. can hominy, drained and rinsed

Place onion in a lightly greased slow cooker; top with beef. Sprinkle with salt. Add green pepper, carrots, celery and garlic to slow cooker. Pour tomatoes with juice and 3/4 cup broth over all. Cover and cook on low setting for 8 hours. In a bowl, mix together cornstarch and remaining broth until smooth; stir into slow cooker during the last 15 minutes of cooking. Stir in hominy and heat through.

Serves 6

PRESNTATION

For a Mexican-inspired fiesta, dress up the table in south-of-the-border style...arrange colorful woven blankets, sombreros and tissue paper flowers around the room!

WILD WEST QUESADILLAS

VICKIE
GOOSEBERY PATCH

On a trip to the southwest, we stopped to camp at a little spot in the middle of nowhere. It was amazing...away from the city lights, the stars shone so bright. This pie-iron recipe was one we enjoyed more than once around the campfire.

Brown ground beef and onion in a large skillet over medium-high heat; drain. Add taco seasoning and water; cook according to package directions. Spray the inside of a pie iron with non-stick vegetable spray; place a tortilla on one side. Spoon about 1/4 cup ground beef mixture on top of tortilla; sprinkle with cheese and top with onion. Place another tortilla on top; close pie iron. Cook over moderate heat until heated through and cheese is melted, about 3 to 6 minutes. Repeat with remaining ingredients to make 5 more. Garnish as desired.

Serves 6

1 lb. ground beef

1/2 c. onion, chopped

1-oz. pkg. taco seasoning mix

3/4 c. water

12 6-inch corn tortillas

1 c. shredded Monterey Jack cheese

Garnish: lettuce, diced tomato, salsa, sour cream

BARBECUED HAMBURGER BUNS

SARA WRIGHT
COLORADO SPRINGS, CO

My husband found this recipe in my grandmother's recipes. We really enjoy the flavors. It's special to have not only her original recipe but the little note my grandfather wrote on it: "Hi, Dreamboat!"

2 lbs. ground beef
1/2 c. onion, finely chopped
1 to 2 cloves garlic, minced
15-oz. can tomato sauce
1/2 c. catsup
1 T. sugar
1 T vinegar
1 T. mustard
8 hamburger buns, split

In a large skillet over medium heat, brown beef with onion and garlic. Drain. Meanwhile, in a saucepan over medium heat, combine remaining ingredients except buns. Stir well and bring to a boil; pour over beef mixture. Simmer until blended well. To serve, spoon beef mixture onto buns.

Serves 8

BILLIE'S SLOPPY JOES

KATHLEEN SIGG
GREELEY, CO

This is my ultimate comfort food, one made by my mom back in the 1950s... now it's my grandchildren's favorite too! The poultry seasoning is the "secret ingredient" that makes the Sloppy Joes so delicious.

1 lb. ground beef
1 onion, chopped
10-3/4 oz. can tomato soup
1 t. chili powder
1/2 t. poultry seasoning
1 t. salt
1/2 t. pepper
1 c. shredded Cheddar cheese
6 hamburger buns, split, toasted and buttered

In a skillet over medium heat, brown ground beef and onion until onion is translucent. Drain; stir in soup and seasonings. Lower heat; cover and simmer for about 30 minutes, stirring occasionally. Stir in cheese and serve on toasted, buttered hamburger buns.

Makes 6 sandwiches

Whether you are looking for a quick-to-make breakfast dish to start the day off right, no-fuss party fare for those special guests, satisfying soups and sandwiches for the perfect lunch, main dishes to bring them to the table fast, or a sweet little something to savor at the end of the meal, you'll love these recipes from the amazing cooks in beautiful Colorado.

Hearty Hominy Beef Stew, p. 78

Dilled Crab Egg Cups, p. 14

Easy Brown Bread, p. 70

Feel-Good Shake, p. 22

Honey-Pumpkin Pie, p. 141

Country Cabin Pancake Syrup, p 18

Orange-Cinnamon French Toast, p. 13

Strawberry-Thyme Jam, p. 22

Luscious Angel Cupcakes, p. 138

Dark Chocolate Pecan Pie, p. 145

Orange-Cranberry Cake, p. 140

Double Chocolate Cookies, p. 139

County Fair Grand Champion Cake, p. 135

Creamy Chicken Bake, p. 106

Colorado Pork Chops, p. 108

Sour Cherry Lattice Pie, p. 144

White Bean & Tomato Salad, p. 48

Kielbasa & Red Beans, p. 107

Perfect Pumpkin-Apple Cake, p. 146

Mack's Honey Apple Rings, p. 45

Savory Beans & Tomatoes Over Rice, p. 35

Lucy's Sausage Salad, p. 47

Swiss Steak Colorado Style, p. 105

COLD-CHASER CHICKEN SOUP

ELISABETH MORRISSEY
DENVER, CO

My friends call me to ask for this recipe whenever they get sick. We've found it clears stuffy noses, opens congested chests, settles the stomach and warms you all over. Pure comfort.

Spray a skillet with non-stick vegetable spray. Add chicken; sauté until no longer pink. Set chicken aside to cool; dice. Meanwhile, in a soup pot over medium-high heat, bring broth to a boil. Stir in vegetables, garlic, ginger and seasonings; reduce heat to low. Cover and simmer for 30 minutes, stirring occasionally. Add diced chicken; cover and simmer for another 30 minutes. Return to a boil; stir in uncooked pasta. Cook over medium-high heat, just until pasta is tender.

Serves 8

2 boneless, skinless chicken breasts

8 c. chicken broth

1 c. onion, diced

2 stalks celery, diced

2 carrots, peeled and diced

6 cloves garlic, minced

1/2 to 1-inch piece fresh ginger, peeled and minced

1 T. poultry seasoning

1 t. red pepper flakes

salt and pepper to taste

1 c. favorite tri-colored vegetable pasta, uncooked

SPICY PORK & HOMINY STEW

RITA MORGAN
PUEBLO, CO

This hearty stew is a snap to put together. If you prefer, combine everything in your slow cooker and cook on low for four hours. I like to serve it with flour tortillas for dipping.

2 lbs. boneless pork loin, cut into 1/2-inch cubes
1 t. oil
1 c. onion, diced
2 cloves garlic, minced
2 15-oz. cans yellow hominy, drained
2 16-oz. cans cannellini beans, drained
10-oz. can diced tomatoes with green chiles
3 4-oz. cans diced green chiles, drained
2 T. chili powder
1 T. ground cumin
1 T. pepper
2 t. dried oregano
salt to taste

In a large Dutch oven over medium heat, brown pork cubes in oil with onion and garlic. Drain; stir in remaining ingredients except salt. Reduce heat to medium-low. Cover and simmer for one hour, stirring occasionally. Season with salt as desired.

Serves 10 to 12

COLORADO HAM & CHEESE

BARBARA DUNCAN
CASTLE ROCK, CO

These can also be assembled, then frozen...just heat as many as needed.

Combine first 5 ingredients; set aside. Mix together chili sauce and mayonnaise; add to ham mixture. Spoon into buns and wrap individually in aluminum foil. Bake at 375 degrees for 15 minutes, or until heated through.

Makes 16 sandwiches

1/2 lb. cooked ham, shredded

1/2 lb. shredded sharp Cheddar cheese

2 eggs, hard-boiled, peeled and finely chopped

1/2 c. onion, finely chopped

1/2 c. green olives with pimentos, finely chopped

1/2 c. chili sauce

3 T. mayonnaise

16 hot dog buns, split

JUST FOR FUN

The slogan of "Pikes Peak or Bust," painted across many of the prairie schooners, was born at a time as fortune hunters headed west. Although only a handful of those who flocked to the region ever found gold.

CHAPTER FOUR

Miner's Meal

Mains

FILL THEM UP WITH
A STICK–TO–THE RIBS MEAL THAT
IS FULL OF FLAVOR AND HEARTY
ENOUGH TO SATISFY EVEN THE
BIGGEST ROCKY MOUNTAIN
APPETITE.

SAVORY PORK RIBS

TIFFANY BRINKLEY
BROOMFIELD, CO

*The sauce is what really makes these ribs stand out
from other recipes. Terrific!*

1/4 c. soy sauce
1/4 c. orange
    marmalade
1 T. catsup
1 clove garlic, pressed
3 to 4 lbs. pork ribs, cut
    into serving-size pieces

Combine soy sauce, marmalade, catsup and garlic;
mix well. Brush over ribs. Arrange in slow cooker;
pour remaining sauce over ribs. Cover and cook on
low setting for 10 to 12 hours.

Serves 6 to 8

HEALTHY CROCK BURRITOS

BARBARA HIGHTOWER
BROOMFIELD, CO

My daughter Gigi gave me this easy recipe for chicken burritos after she served them to us for family dinner at her house. Great for filling up the slow cooker and coming home to a hot meal... they're low-calorie and really delicious!

Arrange chicken breasts in a slow cooker. Layer beans and sauces over chicken. Cover and cook on low setting for 6 to 8 hours. Remove chicken to a plate; shred with a fork. Return chicken to slow cooker and stir to mix. To serve, spoon chicken mixture into tortillas; add desired toppings and roll up.

Serves 4 to 6

4 boneless, skinless chicken breasts

15-oz. can black beans, drained and rinsed

7-oz. can red enchilada sauce

7-oz. can green enchilada sauce

burrito-size flour tortillas

Garnish: chopped onions, shredded lettuce, sour cream, shredded Cheddar cheese

EASY CARNITAS

CHRISTINE ARRIETA
AURORA, CO

When I was a teenager, burritos were my food of choice. My school didn't sell candy at fundraisers, we sold homemade burritos and tortas. My kids like to do the same, but with busy schedules it's not always easy. With this recipe, you can get that traditional flavor without much effort! This flavorful pork can be used to prepare various Mexican dishes.

4 to 5-lb. boneless pork shoulder butt roast

seasoned meat tenderizer

salt and pepper to taste

2 T. olive oil

1/2 onion, chopped

2 cloves garlic, minced

28-oz. can green enchilada sauce

Sprinkle roast generously with tenderizer, salt and pepper; set aside. Heat oil in a large skillet over medium heat. Sauté onion for 2 minutes, or just until translucent. Add garlic; cook for one additional minute. Push onion and garlic to edge of skillet; add roast and brown on all sides. Transfer roast to a large slow cooker; top with onion mixture and enchilada sauce. Cover and cook on low setting for 8 hours, or on high setting for 3 hours, until pork is fork-tender. Shred roast with 2 forks; serve as desired in tacos, burritos and on nachos.

Variation:

For a traditional finish to your carnitas, spoon shredded pork onto an aluminum foil-lined baking sheet. Top with several spoonfuls of sauce. Broil for 5 to 10 minutes, until edges of pork are golden.

Serves 10 to 12

FAST–FIX PENNE ALFREDO

TIFFANY BRINKLEY
BROOMFIELD, CO

So rich and cheesy...a real comfort food for a chilly evening!

Bring a large pot of lightly salted water to a boil. Add pasta and cook for 8 to 10 minutes, until al dente; drain. Combine cream and butter in a Dutch oven over medium-low heat. Cook until butter melts, stirring occasionally; be careful not to bring mixture to a boil. Stir in remaining ingredients. Toss with cooked pasta and serve immediately.

Serves 8

- 16-oz. pkg. penne pasta, uncooked
- 1 c. whipping cream
- 1/2 c. butter, softened
- 1/2 c. grated Parmesan cheese
- 1/2 c. fresh parsley, chopped
- 1 t. salt
- 1/4 t. pepper
- 1/8 t. garlic powder

SPEEDY POTATO PUFF BAKE

CYNDE DUPRE
WINDSOR, CO

A variation on a biscuit-topped casserole, using something my kids ask for again & again...potato puffs! My husband loves this also and requests it often.

In a skillet over medium heat, brown beef, adding onion if desired. Drain. Add soup and beans; stir until combined. Transfer to a greased 2-quart casserole dish. Pat mixture level with the back of a spoon and sprinkle with desired amount of cheese. Arrange potato puffs on top. Bake, uncovered, at 400 degrees until bubbly and puffs have cooked through, about 20 minutes.

Serves 4 to 6

- 1 lb. ground beef
- Optional: 1 onion, diced
- 10-3/4 oz. can cream of mushroom or chicken soup
- 14-1/2 oz. can green beans, drained
- 1 to 2 c. shredded Cheddar cheese
- 26-oz. pkg. extra crispy frozen potato puffs

FIRECRACKER GRILLED SALMON

SHARON DEMERS
DOLORES, CO

*Add more red pepper flakes or a dusting of cayenne pepper for even
more heat!*

4 4 to 6-oz. salmon
   fillets
1/4 c. peanut oil
2 T. soy sauce
2 T. balsamic vinegar
2 T. green onions,
   chopped
1-1/2 t. brown sugar,
   packed
1 clove garlic, minced
1/2 t. red pepper flakes
1/2 t. sesame oil
1/8 t. salt

Place salmon in a glass baking dish. Whisk together
remaining ingredients and pour over salmon.
Cover with plastic wrap; refrigerate for 4 to 6 hours.
Remove salmon, discarding marinade. Place on an
aluminum foil-lined grill that has been sprayed with
non-stick vegetable spray. Grill for 10 minutes per
inch of thickness, measured at thickest part, until
fish flakes when tested with a fork. Turn halfway
through cooking.

Serves 4

COLORADO FUN FACT

Pikes Peak Cog Railway is the highest
railway train in the world. The Pikes Peak
Cog Railway runs on cog wheels and special
track with "teeth" that allow the train to
climb the mountain.

TERIYAKI CHICKEN

LOURY MULHERN
COLORADO SPRINGS, CO

I learned how to make this simple recipe from my cousin's wife from Thailand. It has been a favorite for years. Serve with garlic buttered sautéed vegetables and white or brown rice.

In a large bowl, combine soy sauce, cold water, ginger and garlic. Stir well. Add chicken breasts; turn to coat with sauce. Cover and refrigerate at least 6 hours or overnight for full teriyaki flavor. Drain; discard marinade. Cook on a hot grill at 375 degrees for 20 minutes, or until cooked through and deep golden on both sides. May also be arranged in a shallow 13"x9" baking pan; cover with aluminum foil. Bake at 350 degrees for 30 to 40 minutes.

10-oz. bottle regular or low-sodium soy sauce

1-1/4 c. cold water

5-inch piece ginger root, peeled and diced

4 cloves garlic, chopped

5 boneless, skinless chicken breasts

Serves 5

JUDY'S RED WINE BEEF

HELEN PHILLIPS
EATON, CO

My sister-in-law's friend has Christmas trees all over her house. One year when we went to see her trees, she had this delicious-smelling dinner in the slow cooker. She shared the recipe with us.

Place beef in a 4-quart slow cooker. Pour wine or broth over beef; sprinkle with soup mix. Spoon soup on top. Cover and cook on low setting for 6 to 8 hours, or on high setting for 3 to 4 hours. Serve over cooked rice or egg noodles.

2 lbs. stew beef cubes

1 c. red wine or beef broth

1.35-oz. pkg. onion soup mix

2 10-3/4 oz. cans cream of mushroom soup

cooked rice or egg noodles

Serves 4 to 6

FIESTA CHICKEN SOFT TACOS

MANDY DOOLITTLE
HIGHLANDS RANCH, CO

Family & friends beg me to make these simple and scrumptious tacos. The recipe can easily be doubled to feed a hungry crowd.

2 T. oil

1/2 yellow onion, diced

1/2 green pepper, diced

2 to 3 cloves garlic, minced

1 lb. boneless, skinless chicken breasts, cubed

1 to 2 T. taco seasoning mix

1-1/2 c. chunky salsa

4 6-inch flour tortillas

Garnish: shredded Cheddar cheese or other favorite toppings

Heat oil in a skillet over medium heat. Add onion, green pepper and garlic; sauté until tender. Add chicken; cook until no longer pink, about 5 to 8 minutes. Stir in taco seasoning and salsa; simmer for 3 minutes. To serve, spoon mixture onto tortillas. Fold over once; garnish as desired.

Serves 4

CRANBERRY CORNED BEEF

APRIL JACOBS
LOVELAND, CO

The cranberry glaze against the fresh parsley is so beautiful.

Trim fat from brisket. Place carrots and onion in a slow cooker; place brisket on top of vegetables. Sprinkle spice packet over brisket. Combine cranberry sauces and soup mix in a bowl. Spoon over brisket. Cover and cook on high setting for one hour. Reduce heat to low setting and cook for 8 hours. Meanwhile, combine sour cream and horseradish in a small bowl. Cover and chill until ready to serve. Transfer brisket to a serving platter. Spoon carrots, onion and, if desired, a little cooking liquid around brisket on platter. Serve with sauce. Sprinkle with pepper. Garnish with parsley.

Serves 6 to 8

4-lb. cured corned beef brisket with spice packet

5 large carrots, peeled and cut into 3-inch pieces

1 onion, cut into 6 wedges

14-oz. can whole-berry cranberry sauce

14-oz. can jellied cranberry sauce

2 1-oz. pkgs. onion soup mix

1/2 c. sour cream

4 t. prepared horseradish

1/4 t. pepper

Garnish: fresh parsley, chopped

MOM'S BEEF SOPAPILLAS

ANNE PTACNIK
YUMA, CO

My mom has been making these mouthwatering sopapillas for as long as I can remember. They come out piping-hot and filled with cheesy goodness. Serve on a bed of lettuce...scrumptious!

2 c. all-purpose flour
1 t. baking powder
1 t. salt
1 T. shortening or oil
3/4 c. cold water
1/2 lb. ground beef, browned and drained
salt and pepper to taste
6 slices American cheese
oil for frying
Garnish: sour cream, salsa, sliced black olives, other favorite toppings

Mix flour, baking powder and salt together. In a separate bowl, combine shortening or oil and water; add to flour mixture and stir well. Form dough into 6 balls. Roll each ball into a very thin circle. Spoon about 1/4 cup beef onto the bottom half of each dough circle, leaving 1/2-inch edge of circle without filling. Sprinkle with salt and pepper; top with a cheese slice. Fold top half of dough over the cheese; crimp edges to seal dough around filling. In a Dutch oven over medium-high heat, heat oil to 375 degrees. Fry sopapillas until puffed and golden. Serve hot with desired toppings.

Serves 6

ALL-IN-ONE NOODLE SUPPER

MICHELLE TAGGART
PARKER, CO

My mom started making this comforting one-pot meal when I was a child and I still make it today.

Cook noodles as package directs; drain and set aside. Meanwhile, in a large skillet over medium heat, brown beef. Add onion and cook until tender; drain. Blend in soup, milk and cream cheese; stir in cooked noodles and remaining ingredients. Reduce heat to low. Simmer for 15 to 20 minutes, until heated through and cream cheese is melted.

Serves 6 to 8

8-oz. pkg. wide egg noodles, uncooked

2 lbs. ground beef

1/2 c. onion, chopped

10-3/4 oz. can cream of mushroom soup

3/4 c. milk

8-oz. pkg. cream cheese, cubed and softened

15-3/4 oz. can corn, drained

1-1/2 t. salt

1/8 t. Pepper

TANGY BEEF DIJON

TIFFANY BRINKLEY
BROOMFIELD, CO

*This dish marinates overnight, freeing me up to spend time with family
& friends during their holiday visits.*

1 T. Dijon mustard

**1-1/2 t. prepared
horseradish**

1/4 t. dried basil

1/4 t. dried thyme

1/4 t. dried tarragon

1/4 t. pepper

**2 8-oz. beef tenderloin
steaks**

salt to taste

In a small bowl, stir together mustard, horseradish, basil, thyme, tarragon and pepper. Spread mixture evenly over both sides of steaks. Wrap each steak individually with plastic wrap; refrigerate overnight. When ready to bake, spray a glass 9"x9" baking pan with non-stick vegetable spray. Unwrap steaks and sprinkle with salt. Arrange steaks in baking pan and bake at 400 degrees to desired doneness, 30 minutes for medium-rare, 60 minutes for well-done.

Serves 2

CHILI RELLENO SQUARES

LISA WILLIAMS
LONGMONT, CO

This recipe was always requested for brunch during our moms' group at church.

Spread chiles in the bottom of a greased 13"x9" baking pan. Mix cheeses together and spread over chiles. In a separate bowl, whisk together eggs, evaporated milk and flour; pour over cheeses. Bake at 375 degrees for 30 minutes, or until top is golden. Spread salsa over top and bake an additional 5 to 10 minutes.

Serves 10 to 12

7-oz. can whole or diced green chiles, drained

12-oz. pkg. shredded Colby cheese

12-oz. pkg. shredded Monterey Jack cheese

4 eggs, beaten

12-oz. can evaporated milk

2 T. all-purpose flour

16-oz. jar red or green salsa

PRESNTATION

For buffets or dinner parties, roll up flatware in colorful napkins, tie with ribbon bows and stack in a flat basket. Even kids can help with this well in advance of the party...one less last-minute task!

DIVINE CASSEROLE

**TIFFANY BRINKLEY
BROOMFIELD, CO**

*I like this satisfying casserole with buttery, whipped potatoes...
comfort food!*

8-oz. pkg. egg noodles,
uncooked and divided

1 lb. ground beef

6-oz. can tomato paste

1 t. Worcestershire
sauce

1/4 t. hot pepper sauce

1/8 t. dried oregano

1 onion, chopped

1/2 c. plus 2 T. butter,
melted and divided

8-oz. container small-
curd cottage cheese

1/2 c. sour cream

1/2 c. cream cheese,
softened

Cook noodles according to package directions; drain. Meanwhile, brown beef in a skillet over medium heat; drain. Stir in tomato paste, sauces and oregano; set aside. In a separate skillet, sauté onion in 2 tablespoons butter until tender; place in a bowl. Blend in cottage cheese, sour cream and cream cheese. Place half the noodles in an ungreased 2-quart casserole dish. Drizzle with 1/4 cup melted butter; spread with cheese mixture. Toss remaining noodles with remaining butter; spread over cheese mixture. Top with beef mixture. Bake, uncovered, at 350 degrees for 40 minutes.

Serves 4 to 6

SWISS STEAK COLORADO STYLE

ROBEN BLAKEY
WESTMINSTER, CO

This is one of my husband's favorite go-to meals. We like to eat this as is, but sometimes we spoon it over a baked potato.

Combine all ingredients except cornstarch and water in a freezer-safe container. Refrigerate overnight, or freeze until ready to use.

To cook:

Thaw beef mixture overnight in refrigerator if frozen; spoon into a slow cooker. Cover and cook on low setting for 5 to 6 hours. If a thicker consistency is desired, whisk together cornstarch and water in a cup; drizzle into beef mixture. Cook, uncovered, until thickened.

Serves 4

1-1/2 lb. beef chuck roast

15-oz. can diced tomatoes

1 c. red wine or beef broth

1 T. onion powder

1 t. garlic salt

1 t. pepper

2 carrots, peeled and sliced

1 onion, diced

1/2 to 1 c. beef broth

Optional: 1 T. cornstarch, 1 T. water

CREAMY CHICKEN BAKE

APRIL JACOBS
LOVELAND, CO

*When my picky eaters are away, I'll stir in my favorite ingredients...
mushrooms and chopped green pepper!*

2 c. elbow macaroni,
uncooked

1 c. mayonnaise

10-3/4 oz. can cream of
chicken soup

1-1/2 c. cooked chicken,
chopped

2 c. grated Parmesan
cheese

1/4 c. chopped pimentos

1/4 c. onion, chopped

1/2 c. potato chips,
crushed

Cook macaroni according to package instructions; drain. Meanwhile, in a bowl, combine mayonnaise, soup and chicken. Stir in macaroni and remaining ingredients except potato chips. Transfer to a lightly greased 13"x9" baking pan; sprinkle with potato chips. Bake, uncovered, at 375 degrees for 30 minutes, or until bubbly.

Serves 4 to 6

KIELBASA & RED BEANS

BETH SCHLIEPER
LAKEWOOD, CO

Serve over bowls of rice for traditional red beans & rice.

Combine all ingredients in a slow cooker. Cover and cook on low setting for 8 hours, or on high setting for 4 to 5 hours.

Serves 6 to 8

1 lb. Kielbasa, cut into bite-size pieces

4 to 5 16-oz. cans red beans, drained and rinsed

2 14-1/2 oz. cans diced tomatoes

1 onion, chopped

hot pepper sauce to taste

COLORADO PORK CHOPS

LINDA WOLFE
WESTMINSTER, CO

These tasty pork chops feature all the flavors of your favorite Mexican restaurant.

6 bone-in pork chops, 1-1/2 inches thick

15-oz. can chili beans with chili sauce

1-1/2 c. salsa

1 c. corn

Optional: green chiles to taste

cooked rice

Garnish: fresh cilantro

In a slow cooker, layer pork chops, beans, salsa, corn and chiles, if using. Cover and cook on low setting for 5 hours, or on high setting for 2-1/2 hours. Serve over cooked rice; garnish with cilantro.

Serves 6

AMIGO TACO BAKE

BOBBIE KEEFER
BYERS, CO

This is a true Tex-Mex version of a taco casserole and a great recipe for a beginner cook. When I first saw the ingredients, I thought the cream of mushroom soup was a weird ingredient for a Mexican dish, but it works! Serve with diced tomato, shredded lettuce, sliced jalapeños or any favorite burrito toppings. I make guacamole salad to go with this dish and serve it with extra corn chips.

Brown beef with onion in a skillet over medium-high heat; drain. In a bowl, stir together soup, tomatoes and reserved bean juice. To assemble, spread corn chips in a buttered 13"x9" baking pan. Layer beef mixture and beans over the chips. Spread soup mixture on top. Cover with cheese. Bake, uncovered, at 350 degrees for 30 to 40 minutes, until bubbly and golden. Serve with salsa and sour cream.

Serves 6

1 lb. lean ground beef

1 c. onion, diced

10-3/4 oz. can cream of mushroom soup

10-oz. can diced tomatoes with mild or spicy green chiles

15-oz. can ranch-style beans, drained and juice reserved

3 c. corn chips, crushed

8-oz. pkg. shredded Cheddar Jack cheese

Garnish: salsa, sour cream

COLORADO SKI CHILI BAKE

SANDRA SULLIVAN
AURORA, CO

This is a recipe that Great-Grandma made for us when we came in from skiing. So easy and so good!

3 lbs. ground beef
3/4 c. onion, chopped
15-oz. can tomato soup
15-oz. can tomato sauce
1 T. vinegar
2 T. chili powder
1 t. salt
1/2 t. pepper
1/4 t. garlic powder
4 15-oz. cans kidney
   beans, drained and
   rinsed

In a large skillet over medium heat, brown beef and onion; drain. Stir in soup, sauce, vinegar and seasonings. Simmer over medium-low heat until heated through. Add kidney beans to a Dutch oven; pour beef mixture over top. Bake, uncovered, at 350 degrees for one hour, or until heated through, adding a little water if mixture gets too dry.

Serves 10 to 12

DINNERTIME CONVERSATION

"Beulah red" is the name of the red marble that gives the State Capitol its distinctive color. Cutting, polishing, and installing the marble took six years (from 1894 to 1900). All the Beulah red marble in the world went into the Capitol and it cannot be replaced at any price.

GREEN CHILE BAKED BURRITOS

DANIELLE STENGER
ORCHARD, CO

I created this recipe one afternoon when I wanted burritos smothered with green chile, but did not have the time to make a batch of green chile sauce. This instantly became a family favorite! I get special requests for these burritos whenever I am having company over. It is a fairly easy dish and makes the house smell wonderful.

Prepare rice mix according to package directions; set aside. Meanwhile, brown beef in a skillet over medium heat; drain. Stir in taco seasoning,water and chiles. Simmer over medium heat until sauce is thickened. Reduce to low heat. Stir in beans; mix well and heat through. To each tortilla, add one cup beef mixture, 1/3 cup Spanish rice and 3 tablespoons shredded cheese. Roll up tortillas and tuck in ends; place in a lightly greased 13"x9" baking pan. Spoon enchilada sauce over burritos; top with remaining cheese. Bake, uncovered, at 375 degrees for 30 minutes, or until heated through and cheese is melted. Garnish as desired.

Serves 6

7-oz. pkg. Spanish rice mix

1 lb. ground beef

1-1/4 oz. pkg. taco seasoning mix

3/4 c. water

4-oz. can diced green chiles

16-oz. can refried beans

6 burrito-size flour tortillas

3 c. shredded Cheddar cheese, divided

15-oz. can green chile enchilada sauce

Optional: guacamole, sour cream, diced tomatoes, green onions

CREAMED HAM ON CORNBREAD

CARA LORENZ
OLATHE, CO

This is an old-fashioned meal that is budget-friendly. My family really enjoys the different flavors as a change of pace from meat & potato main dishes.

8-1/2 oz. pkg. corn muffin mix
1/3 c. milk
1 egg, beaten
2 T. butter
2 T. all-purpose flour
1/4 t. salt
1-1/2 c. milk
3/4 c. shredded Cheddar cheese
1-1/2 c. cooked ham, cubed

Combine muffin mix, milk and egg; mix well and pour into a greased 8"x8" baking pan. Bake at 400 degrees for 18 to 20 minutes. In a saucepan, melt butter over low heat. Stir in flour and salt. Slowly add milk, whisking until smooth. Bring to a boil; boil and stir for 2 minutes. Stir in cheese and ham; heat through. Cut cornbread into squares; top with creamed ham.

Serves 4

PORK TENDERLOIN WITH ROASTED GRAPES

TIFFANY BRINKLEY
BROOMFIELD, CO

Your guests will be wowed by this dish...they'll never guess it was so easy to prepare.

In a bowl, stir together fennel seed, salt and pepper. Rub mixture over tenderloin; set aside. In an oven-proof skillet, cook tenderloin in oil 5 minutes, turning to brown all sides. Add grapes and broth to skillet; heat to boiling. Cover and bake at 475 degrees until fully cooked, about 15 to 18 minutes. Transfer pork to a platter and keep warm. Return skillet with grape mixture to stovetop; bring to a boil over high heat. Cook and stir until liquid has thickened, about one minute. Slice pork; serve with grapes and sauce from the skillet.

Serves 4

1 t. fennel seed, crushed
1/2 t. salt
1/2 t. pepper
1-lb. pork tenderloin
2 t. olive oil
1-1/2 c. seedless red grapes
1-1/2 c. seedless green grapes
1/2 c. chicken broth

PESTO–BRIE GRILLED CHICKEN

BRENDA SCHLOSSER
BRIGHTON, CO

A dish I came up with just for the love of basil and brie together. Serve with angel hair pasta tossed with olive oil, sun-dried tomatoes and fresh garlic...wonderful!

4 boneless, skinless chicken breasts
1/4 c. basil pesto sauce
4 slices brie cheese, 1/4-inch thick
salt and pepper to taste

Place chicken on an oiled grate over medium-high heat. Grill for 3 to 5 minutes; turn chicken over. Spread each piece with one tablespoon pesto and top with a cheese slice. Cover; continue cooking for 3 to 5 minutes, until cheese is melted and chicken juices run clear.

Serves 4

CHICKEN ENCHILADA BAKE

SARA WRIGHT
COLORADO SPRINGS, CO

One evening I was in the mood for Mexican food, but didn't have any taco shells or tortillas in the pantry. I decided to try using pasta...my family really enjoyed this new dish!

2 c. rotini pasta, uncooked
1 lb. boneless, skinless chicken breasts, cooked and chopped
15-oz. can diced tomatoes, drained
1-1/2 c. shredded Mexican-blend cheese, divided
10-oz. can enchilada sauce

Cook pasta according to package directions; drain. In a large bowl, combine cooked pasta, chicken, tomatoes and one cup cheese; stir in enchilada sauce. Spoon into a greased 2-quart casserole dish. Bake, uncovered, at 350 degrees for 20 to 25 minutes, until heated through and cheese is melted. Top with remaining cheese. Return to oven an additional 2 to 3 minutes, until cheese is melted.

Serves 4

FISH MEETS CHIPS

SANDRA SULLIVAN
AURORA, CO

I love crispy fish but don't want to fry it...this is a tasty alternative.

Mix crushed chips with thyme in a shallow dish; set aside. Pat fish fillets dry with paper towels. Brush both sides of fish with salad dressing or mayonnaise; coat fish on both sides with chip mixture. Arrange fish on an aluminum foil-lined baking sheet that has been sprayed with non-stick vegetable spray. Bake, uncovered, at 450 degrees for 6 to 10 minutes, until fish flakes easily with a fork.

Serves 4

4 c. potato chips, crushed

1/2 t. dried thyme

4 fillets cod, tilapia or perch, 1/2 to 3/4 inch thick, thawed if frozen

2/3 c. honey-mustard salad dressing or mayonnaise

CAPE COD SUMMER SCALLOPS

SANDRA SULLIVAN
AURORA, CO

We spend summers on Cape Cod with friends and this is similar to a dish served at a quaint little fish restaurant. The dish is so simple and fresh...with a salad, it makes for a delightful summer evening.

6-oz. pkg. herb-flavored dressing mix

1 T. seafood seasoning

2 6-oz. cans chopped clams

1 doz. large sea scallops, cleaned and patted dry

4 T. butter, sliced

Garnish: lemon wedges

Prepare dressing mix according to package directions; stir in seasoning and clams with juice. Spray 4 large scallop shells or individual ramekins with non-stick butter spray. Divide dressing mixture evenly among dishes; top with scallops, dividing evenly. Top each with one tablespoon butter. Set dishes on a baking sheet. Bake, uncovered, at 425 degrees for 15 to 20 minutes. Serve with lemon wedges.

Serves 4

MEXICAN TURKEY DRUMSTICKS

APRIL JACOBS
LOVELAND, CO

One Thanksgiving, my husband was away on military duty, and my kids & I didn't feel like having the traditional turkey dinner. I found this recipe, and it was perfect! The kids got to eat their drumsticks with their hands, and we enjoyed Spanish rice and black beans on the side. Such fun...making memories of a different kind!

Place drumsticks in a lightly greased 6-quart slow cooker; set aside. Combine remaining ingredients except cornstarch and cold water in a bowl; spoon over drumsticks. Cover and cook on low setting for 8 to 10 hours. Remove drumsticks to a platter; keep warm. Strain sauce in slow cooker into a saucepan. Combine cornstarch and water until smooth; stir into sauce in pan. Bring to a boil over medium heat; cook and stir for 2 minutes, or until thickened. Serve drumsticks with sauce.

Serves 4 to 6

4 to 6 turkey drumsticks

10-oz. can enchilada sauce

4-oz. can chopped green chiles

1 t. dried oregano

1/2 t. ground cumin

1/2 t. garlic salt

3 T. cornstarch

3 T. cold water

CHAPTER FIVE

GOLD NUGGET
Appetizers
& Snacks

WHETHER YOU ARE HAVING
COMPANY OR JUST NEED A SNACK
TO HOLD YOU OVER UNTIL
THE NEXT MEAL, THESE LITTLE
NUGGETS ARE GOOD AS GOLD AND
ARE SURE TO BECOME FAVORITE
GO-TO APPETIZERS.

PEPPER JELLY CREAM CHEESE

HOLLY CHILD
PARKER, CO

With just a few ingredients on hand, I can always whip up this quick appetizer for any type of gathering. Easy to put together and always a big hit with its spicy-sweet flavor.

8-oz. pkg. cream cheese, softened
1/4 c. medium salsa
1/4 c. orange marmalade
assorted crackers

Unwrap cream cheese and place the block on a serving dish. Mix together salsa and marmalade in a bowl; spoon evenly over cream cheese. Serve with assorted crackers.

Serves 10

DINNERTIME CONVERSATION

Colorado once had 3 Governors in a single day. On March 17, 1905, Democrat Alva Adams was forced to resign because of election improprieties (one district had 717 votes for Adams but only 100 registered voters). He was replaced by Republican James H. Peabody, who had run against him in the election, on the condition that he immediately resign. He did so, yielding to his Lieutenant Governor, Jesse F. McDonald.

CHEESY MEXICAN BEAN DIP

TAMMY NAVARRO
LITTLETON, CO

I love cheese dip and also love bean dip...this combines both. It's yummy! Use your favorite salsa. Serve with tortilla chips.

Combine all ingredients in a 3-quart slow cooker; do not drain corn. Stir well. Cover and cook on low setting for one to 2 hours, until heated through. Stir again; serve warm.

Serves 10

10-3/4 oz. can nacho cheese soup

11-oz. can sweet corn and diced peppers

16-oz. jar favorite salsa

9-oz. can mild or spicy bean dip

3/4 c. regular or non-alcoholic beer

PINE CONE CHEESE BALL

DIANA LAMPHERE
COLORADO SPRINGS, CO

A basic cheese ball, but very good. It's pretty served on a faux pine bough...takes a little time to arrange the almonds, but it's worth it. Rave reviews! You can also decorate it in many other ways. Roll it in chopped walnuts or pecans, or make it into a snowman.

In a large bowl, combine all ingredients except almonds; blend well. Shape into a large egg shape; place on a serving plate. Layer with sliced almonds in rows to resemble a pine cone. Cover and refrigerate until serving time.

Makes one large cheese ball.

1-1/2 c. cream cheese, softened

1/2 c. grated Parmesan cheese

1/4 c. mayonnaise

1/2 t. dried oregano

1/8 t. garlic salt, or to taste

6-oz. pkg. sliced almonds

JALAPEÑO POPPER DIP

ANNE PTACNIK
YUMA, CO

I love making jalapeño poppers, but was looking for an alternative that took less time. So I combined all the ingredients in my small slow cooker and served with tortilla chips for dipping. I brought it to my bunco group and the ladies loved it! A few days later, my husband asked me to make it for our family, too.

8-oz. pkg. cream cheese, softened

8-oz. pkg. shredded sharp Cheddar cheese

1/3 c. sour cream

1/3 c. mayonnaise

1/8 t. garlic powder

1/8 t. salt

1/8 t. pepper

3 jalapeño peppers, seeded and finely diced

6 to 8 slices bacon, crisply cooked and crumbled

tortilla or corn chips

In a bowl, combine all ingredients except bacon and chips; stir well to combine. Transfer to a greased 3-quart slow cooker. Cover and cook on low setting for 3 to 4 hours, until hot and cheeses are melted. Stir; top with bacon and stir again to partially combine. Serve with tortilla or corn chips.

Serves 6 to 8

SPINACH–ARTICHOKE CHILE DIP

MARLA KINNERSLEY
HIGHLANDS RANCH, CO

This recipe is requested time & time again whenever we get together with friends. Green chiles really add something special to its flavor and it goes quickly at gatherings.

In a bowl, combine spinach, artichokes, chiles, cheeses, mayonnaise and seasonings. Mix together well. Spoon into an ungreased one-quart casserole dish. Bake at 375 degrees for about 20 minutes, until hot and lightly golden on top. Serve with tortilla chips, veggies or bread.

Serves 6

- 10-oz. pkg. frozen chopped spinach, thawed and drained
- 14-oz. can artichoke hearts, drained and chopped
- 2 4-oz. cans chopped green chiles, drained
- 8-oz. pkg. light cream cheese, softened
- 1/2 c. shredded Parmesan cheese
- 1/2 c. mayonnaise
- 1/4 t. garlic salt
- 1/8 t. salt
- 1/8 t. pepper
- tortilla chips, carrot and celery sticks, bread slices

SALMON CHEESE BALL

DANIELLE STENGER
ORCHARD, CO

*Our whole family has a large Christmas Eve get-together every year,
and I always make this cheese ball for it. Even the kids love it!*

14-3/4 oz. can salmon,
drained

8-oz. pkg. cream cheese,
softened

1 T. smoke-flavored
cooking sauce

3/4 c. onion, diced

dried parsley to taste

assorted crackers

Pick through salmon, discarding any bones. Transfer to a large bowl and flake with a fork. Add cream cheese, sauce and onion; blend well. Lay out a piece of plastic wrap; sprinkle parsley generously all over plastic wrap. Spoon salmon mixture out onto plastic wrap. Gather plastic wrap around mixture; place into a bowl. Wrap mixture tightly; form to the bowl. Refrigerate for at least one hour. Lift cheese ball out of bowl; unwrap onto a serving plate and surround with assorted crackers.

Serves 10

GREEN CHILE CHICKEN DIP

HOLLY CHILD
PARKER, CO

*I first tried this recipe at a potluck at work, years & years ago. I decided to
make it and try it out on my boyfriend Jeff, who later became my husband.
To this day, it is still his very favorite treat, and he makes it for any
occasion, big or small.*

12-1/2 oz. can chicken,
drained

2 8-oz. pkgs. cream
cheese, softened and
cubed

4-oz. can diced jalapeño
peppers

2 4-oz. cans diced green
chiles

2 10-3/4 oz. cans cream
of chicken soup

tortilla chips

In a slow cooker, combine all ingredients except chips; do not drain peppers or chiles. Stir until well blended. Cover and cook on low setting for 3 to 4 hours, stirring occasionally. Serve warm with tortilla chips.

Serves 10 to 12

NUTS & BOLTS

DENISE NEAL
CASTLE ROCK, CO

This is a favorite from a wooden box of recipes my sister-in-law Miranda gave me. The recipes are handwritten and yellowed with age, just the way I like them. I've never seen this version of this snack before. It's great to heap up in a large bowl for games or holiday parties.

In a large saucepan over low heat, melt butter with Worcestershire sauce and spices. Stir well; remove from heat. In an ungreased large roasting pan, combine remaining ingredients. Drizzle butter mixture over cereal mixture; toss to coat well. Bake, uncovered, at 225 degrees for 2 hours, stirring every 20 minutes. Stir well; cool before serving. Store in a covered container.

Makes 15 to 20 servings

3 c. butter

1-1/2 T. Worcestershire sauce

1-1/2 t. garlic salt

1-1/2 t. onion salt

12-oz. pkg. bite-size crispy wheat cereal squares

12-oz. pkg. bite-size crispy rice cereal squares

12-oz. pkg. bite-size crispy corn cereal squares

9-oz. pkg. shredded wheat crackers

6-oz. pkg. thin pretzel sticks, rings or mini twists

1 c. peanuts or other nuts, as desired

KITCHEN TIP

A dash of cider vinegar adds zing to any cabbage dish.

CRAB & GRAPEFRUIT COCKTAIL

KATHY DAYNES
LITTLETON, CO

This is a recipe that my mother-in-law Tony would serve on Christmas Eve. It is an unusual recipe, one that most people haven't ever tried. It's so delicious, some might require a spoon! For the best flavor, refrigerate for the full twenty-four hours.

46-oz. can tomato juice
24-oz. bottle catsup
juice of 2 lemons
6-oz. can crabmeat, well drained
2 c. grapefruit sections, cut into bite-size pieces
salt and pepper to taste
shredded wheat crackers

Mix together all ingredients except crackers in a large bowl. Cover and chill 4 to 24 hours. Serve with shredded wheat crackers.

Serves 12

TORTELLINI & PESTO DIP

BARB FULTON
ARVADA, CO

Whenever I need a dish to bring to a potluck or gathering, this is a great one! It's a little more than chips and it's not dessert. We also like to use the dip to fill multicolored little mini sweet peppers. For a yummy variation, use crumbled goat cheese instead of cream cheese.

2 9-oz. pkgs. refrigerated cheese tortellini, uncooked
7-oz. jar basil pesto sauce
8-oz. pkg. cream cheese, softened
1 t. lemon juice

Cook tortellini according to package directions; drain and cool. Meanwhile, in a bowl, mix together pesto, cream cheese and lemon juice. Chill dip and tortellini separately. Serve tortellini alongside dip.

Serves 10 to 12

KATHIE'S PACKS–A–PUNCH SNACK MIX

KATHIE LORENZINI
IGNACIO, CO

I like to take this on trips in the car...it provides lots of energy and is good for you too!

Combine all ingredients in a large bowl. Store in an airtight container, or place in little snack-size containers for easy toting.

Serves 24

8-oz. pkg. fish-shaped pretzel crackers

1/2 c. whole almonds, toasted

1/2 c. hazelnuts, chopped

4-oz. pkg. dried blueberries

5-1/2 oz. pkg. dried cherries

1/2 c. sweetened dried cranberries

1/2 c. dried apricots, halved

1/2 c. chopped dates

SPICY CRANBERRY MEATBALLS

KATIE SEEST
DENVER, CO

My teen sons enjoy these meatballs in sandwiches, as a snack or even over pasta. They are sweet and spicy.

Combine sauces and brown sugar in a 5-quart slow cooker; stir to mix well. Add meatballs; stir to coat thoroughly with sauce. Cover and cook on low setting for 4 hours.

Makes 12 servings

2 14-oz. cans whole-berry cranberry sauce

2 12-oz. jars General Tso's sauce

1/2 c. brown sugar, packed

2 26-oz. pkg's. frozen homestyle meatballs

AUNT BARB'S DIP

**BRITTNEY GREEN
FREDERICK, CO**

This dip has been a favorite in our family for years...everyone just loves it! It's perfect for fall football parties. You can easily double the recipe, and you very well may need to.

**1-1/2 lbs. ground beef
1 onion, chopped
1 green pepper, chopped
1 T. chili powder
14-1/2 oz. can stewed
  tomatoes
15-oz. can ranch-style
  pinto beans with
  jalapeños
10-3/4 oz. can cream of
  chicken soup
10-3/4 oz. can cream of
  mushroom soup
16-oz. pkg. pasteurized
  process cheese spread,
  cubed
tortilla chips**

In a skillet over medium heat, brown beef with onion and green pepper; drain. Sprinkle with chili powder. Transfer beef mixture to a large slow cooker; add undrained tomatoes, undrained beans and remaining ingredients except tortilla chips. Stir well. Cover and cook on low setting for 4 hours, stirring occasionally, until cheese melts and dip is warmed through. Serve warm with tortilla chips.

Serves 20

COLORADO FUN FACT

In Denver, you can attend sporting events for the NFL (Broncos), MLB (Rockies), NHL (Avalanche), and the NBA (Nuggets) all within a three-mile radius!

SNOWY TRAIL MIX

HEATHER PLASTERER
COLORADO SPRINGS, CO

Pick up a pack of white paper lunch sacks and wrap up a lot of sweet gifts in a hurry. Simply fill the bags with goodies, fold over the tops twice and add a brightly colored sticker...done! So easy and so yummy! I have given it in little cellophane bags tied with a cute ribbon for gifts...everybody loves them.

In a large microwave-safe bowl, mix all ingredients except white chocolate; set aside. Place white chocolate in a separate microwave-safe bowl. Microwave chocolate on high for one to 2 minutes; stir until smooth. Slowly pour melted chocolate over pretzel mixture, gently stirring until evenly covered with chocolate. Scoop out onto wax paper. Let cool 20 minutes; break into bite-size clusters.

Makes 10 cups

3 c. mini pretzel sticks
1-1/2 c. bite-size corn & rice cereal squares
3/4 c. pecan halves
1/2 c. sweetened dried cranberries
1/2 c. cashew halves
1 c. red and green candy-coated chocolates
12-oz. pkg. white melting chocolate, chopped

STUFFED MUSHROOMS

LINDA HARRIS
COLORADO SPRINGS, CO

I received this recipe from a friend many years ago. They are a cinch to make and a family favorite at holiday parties. Be repared to share the recipe...they are delicious!

Brown sausage in a skillet over medium-high heat; drain. Transfer to a bowl and combine with cream cheese, using a fork to blend thoroughly. Place a rounded teaspoonful of sausage mixture inside each mushroom cap. Place on lightly greased baking sheets. Bake at 350 degrees for 20 to 25 minutes, until heated through.

Makes about 2-1/2 dozen

1 lb. sage-flavored ground pork sausage
8-oz. pkg. cream cheese, softened
25 to 30 small whole button mushrooms, stems removed

CHAPTER SIX

Railroad Depot

Desserts

THERE IS ALWAYS ROOM FOR
DESSERT. SO WHETHER YOUR SWEET
TOOTH IS CALLING OR THE TRAIN'S
A-COMING, THESE SIMPLE SWEETS
ARE THE PERFECT TREAT TO TAKE
ALONG OR TO END THE DAY.

GRANDMA'S APPLE-NUT DESSERT

CINDY PUGLIESE
WHEAT RIDGE, CO

When my sister Linda and I were growing up, this dessert was served alongside the pumpkin pie on Thanksgiving. We associate this recipe with our grandma, but the recipe originally came from our dad's grandma. Now Linda hosts Thanksgiving, and she always asks me to bring this dessert. It's easy to make and very good!

1-1/2 c. sugar
1 c. all-purpose flour
2 t. baking powder
1/2 t. salt
2 eggs, beaten
1 t. vanilla extract
2 c. tart apples, cored
  and chopped
1 c. walnuts, coarsely
  chopped
Garnish: whipped cream

Blend together sugar, flour, baking powder and salt in a large bowl. Add remaining ingredients except whipped cream; stir well. Spread in a greased 12"x9" baking pan. Bake, uncovered, at 350 degrees for 30 minutes. Serve topped with dollops of whipped cream.

Serves 12

NANA'S YUMMY RICE PUDDING

SANDRA SULLIVAN
AURORA, CO

How easy is this for evening dessert? My Nana gave me this recipe, and it is oh-so good...comfort food for everyone.

In a saucepan over medium heat, heat milk just until boiling; remove from heat. In a bowl, combine hot milk, rice and remaining ingredients; mix well. Spoon mixture into a lightly greased slow cooker. Cover and cook on high setting for 1-1/2 to 2 hours, stirring often during the last 30 minutes of cooking.

Serves 6

1-1/2 c. milk
1-3/4 c. instant rice, uncooked
2/3 c. brown sugar, packed
1 T. butter, softened
2 t. vanilla extract
1/2 t. nutmeg
3 eggs
1 c. raisins

BONUS IDEA

A fun way to invite guests over... fill bouquets of balloons with helium and write the who, what and where party information on each with a permanent pen. Hand deliver or tie securely to doorknobs with lengths of curling ribbon.

ANGEL FOOD PINEAPPLE CAKE

SANDRA SULLIVAN
AURORA, CO

A great last-minute dessert! In no time at all, I can whip this up and serve it with a bowl of fresh berries and some creamy topping.

16-oz. pkg. angel food cake mix

20-oz. can crushed pineapple

Garnish: assorted fresh berries, whipped cream

Pour dry cake mix into a large bowl; add pineapple with juice. Mix well; batter will begin to foam. Spread batter in a 13"x9" baking pan lightly sprayed with non-stick vegetable spray. Bake at 350 degrees for 30 minutes. Cut into squares; top with berries and a dollop of whipped cream.

Serves 12

BLUEBERRY BREAD PUDDING

RITA MORGAN
BROOFIELD, CO

I love this recipe for get-togethers. It's the perfect recipe to take to bonfires or potlucks because it can be cooked in the slow cooker. My husband loves it served with vanilla icecream.

2 cups frozen blueberries

1 tbsp flour

8 cups French bread cubed

4 eggs

¾ cup milk

¼ cup pure maple syrup

1 cup half-n-half

2 tsp vanilla

3 tsp ground cinnamon

½ cup brown sugar

½ cup granulated sugar

In a bowl, coat frozen blueberries with flour. Whisk together eggs, milk, maple syrup, half-and-half, vanilla, cinnamon, brown sugar and granulated sugar. Place bread cubes and blueberries in a large greased slow cooker; drizzle egg mixture over bread mixture. Stir to coat evenly. Cook on low for 3-4 hours.

Serves 6

COUNTY FAIR GRAND CHAMPION CAKE

CINDY CONWAY
ELIZABETH, CO

*You'll never believe the surprise ingredient that makes this cake a winner...
it's beets!*

Mix together flour, baking soda and salt; set aside. Melt chocolate with 1/4 cup oil in a double boiler; set aside. Purée beets in a blender; measure 2 cups and set aside. Blend sugar and eggs in a large bowl; gradually mix in remaining oil, pureéd beets, melted chocolate and vanilla. Stir in flour mixture; mix well. Grease a Bundt® pan and dust with cocoa; pour batter into pan. Bake at 375 degrees for one hour, or until a toothpick tests clean. Cool for 15 minutes on a wire rack. Turn out cake; dust with powdered sugar.

Serves 10 to 12

- 2 c. all-purpose flour
- 2 t. baking soda
- 1/4 t. salt
- 3 1-oz. sqs. semi-sweet baking chocolate
- 1 c. oil, divided
- 2 15-oz. cans sliced beets, drained
- 1-3/4 c. sugar
- 3 eggs, beaten
- 1 t. vanilla extract
- Garnish: baking cocoa, powdered sugar

BONUS IDEA

Have fun with party invitations... hand deliver the details rolled up in a small glass bottle or write them on the "tail" of a party blower.

RANGER COOKIES

**HEATHER PLASTERER
COLORADO SPRINGS, CO**

The scrumptious taste of these crunchy cookies will always take me back home. Mom made them often while we were growing up and took them along to lots of get-togethers. Yum!

1 c. shortening
1 c. sugar
1 c. brown sugar, packed
2 eggs, beaten
1 t. vanilla extract
2 c. all-purpose flour
1 t. baking powder
1 t. baking soda
1/2 t. salt
2 c. long-cooking oats, uncooked
2 c. crispy rice cereal
1 c. sweetened flaked coconut

In a large bowl, blend together shortening and sugars; beat in eggs and vanilla. In a separate bowl, mix together flour, baking powder, baking soda and salt; stir in oats, cereal and coconut. Add flour mixture to shortening mixture; mix well. Drop by rounded teaspoonfuls onto ungreased baking sheets. Bake at 350 degrees for 10 minutes.

Makes 2-1/2 dozen

JUST FOR FUN

The world's largest flat-top mountain is the Grand Mesa near Grand Junction.

MOM'S WACKY CAKE

SANDY UNREIN
LITTLETON, CO

My mom always made this cake...it's so simple. The texture is between a cake and a brownie, and it needs absolutely no frosting. The flavor improves as the days go by, plus, it's fun to make with the kids!

Sift together flour, sugar, cocoa, baking soda and salt in an ungreased 13"x9" baking pan. Make 3 wells in flour mixture. Add oil to one well, vinegar to another well and vanilla to the remaining well. Drizzle water over all; mix well. Bake at 350 degrees for 35 minutes, or until a toothpick inserted in the center tests clean.

Serves 16

3 c. cake flour
2 c. sugar
6 T. baking cocoa
2 t. baking soda
1 t. salt
3/4 c. oil
2 T. white vinegar
2 t. vanilla extract
2 c. water

LUSCIOUS ANGEL CUPCAKES

SANDRA SULLIVAN
AURORA, CO

These are our favorite summer birthday treats...they're great to take to picnics or to a poolside party.

16-oz. pkg. angel food cake mix

3.4-oz. pkg instant vanilla pudding mix

2 8-oz. cans crushed pineapple

1 c. frozen whipped topping, thawed

2 c. assorted fresh berries

Prepare cake mix as directed on the package. Pour batter into 24 to 30 paper-lined muffin cups, filling each 2/3 full. Bake at 375 degrees for 12 to 15 minutes, until tops are golden and a toothpick tests clean. Cool cupcakes in pan for 10 minutes; remove to wire racks to cool completely. In a bowl, mix together dry pudding mix and undrained pineapple. Gently fold in whipped topping; spread evenly over cupcakes. Top each cupcake with berries; store in refrigerator until ready to serve.

Makes 2 dozen

DOUBLE CHOCOLATE COOKIES

KRISTI WATSON
HIGHLAND RANCH, CO

Doubly delectable! For variety, use white chocolate chips.

In a large bowl, mix sugar, brown sugar, butter and eggs. In another bowl, whisk remaining ingredients except chocolate chips and garnish. Add flour mixture to sugar mixture and combine until well blended. Stir in chocolate chips. Form dough into one-inch balls; roll in additional sugar. Place on ungreased baking sheets. Bake at 350 degrees for 8 to 10 minutes.

Makes 3 dozen

1 c. sugar
1 c. brown sugar, packed
1 c. butter, softened
2 eggs, beaten
1 t. baking soda
1 t. cream of tartar
1/2 t. salt
2 c. all-purpose flour
1/2 c. baking cocoa
1 c. semi-sweet chocolate chips
Garnish: additional sugar

ORANGE-CRANBERRY CAKE

TIFFANY BRINKLEY
BROOMFIELD, CO

My book club friends ask me to make this when it's my turn to host!

- 18-1/2 oz. pkg. white cake mix
- 3.4-oz. pkg. instant vanilla pudding mix
- 1 t. orange zest
- 1/2 c. butter, melted and cooled
- 4 eggs, beaten
- 1 c. milk
- 1-1/2 c. cranberries, chopped
- 1 c. dried apricots, coarsely chopped

Orange Glaze
- 1 c. vanilla frosting
- 1 T. frozen orange juice concentrate, thawed

Combine dry cake mix, dry pudding mix and orange zest. Add melted butter, eggs and milk; beat according to cake package directions. Fold in cranberries and apricots. Spoon batter into a lightly greased tube pan. Bake at 350 degrees for 55 to 65 minutes, or until a toothpick tests clean. Cool in pan for 20 minutes. Remove from pan and cool completely. Drizzle with Orange Glaze.

Orange Glaze:
Stir ingredients together in a microwave-safe bowl. Microwave on medium power for 30 to 45 seconds, or until glaze is desired consistency.

Serves 12

COLORADO FUN FACT

Colorado is nicknamed the "Centennial State" because it became a state in the year 1876. That's 100 years after the signing of the Declaration of Independence.

HONEY-PUMPKIN PIE

SHARON DEMERS
DOLORES, CO

Whenever I can, I make this pie with farm-fresh eggs and honey from a local beekeeper.

Stir together pumpkin, honey, salt and spices in a large bowl. Add eggs and mix well; stir in both milks. Place pie crust in a 9" pie plate; flute edges, forming a high rim to hold pumpkin filling. Do not pierce crust. Place pie plate on oven rack; pour in filling. Bake at 375 degrees for 55 to 60 minutes, or until set. Let cool before serving.

Serves 6 to 8

15-oz. can pumpkin
3/4 c. honey
1/2 t. salt
1 t. cinnamon
1/2 t. ground ginger
1/4 t. ground cloves
1/4 t. nutmeg
3 eggs, beaten
2/3 c. evaporated milk
1/2 c. milk
9-inch pie crust

COOL MINT CHOCOLATE SWIRLS

APRIL JACOBS
LOVELAND, CO

These chocolatey cookies are irresistibly delicious with a cup of hot coffee.

3/4 c. butter

1-1/2 c. brown sugar, packed

2 T. water

12-oz. pkg. semi-sweet chocolate chips

2 eggs

2-1/2 c. all-purpose flour

1-1/4 t. baking soda

1/2 t. salt

2 4.67-oz. pkgs. crème de menthe chocolate wafers

Combine butter, brown sugar and water in a large saucepan. Cook over medium heat, stirring occasionally, until butter melts and mixture is smooth. Remove from heat. Add chocolate chips, stirring until melted; cool 10 minutes. Pour chocolate mixture into a large bowl. Add eggs, one at a time, stirring until well blended; set aside. Combine flour, baking soda and salt in a separate bowl, stirring to mix. Add flour mixture to chocolate mixture, stirring well. Cover and chill one hour. Shape dough into walnut-size balls; place 2 inches apart on greased baking sheets. Bake at 350 degrees for 8 to 10 minutes, being careful not to overbake. Press one crème de menthe wafer onto each warm cookie and let stand one minute; use the back of a spoon to swirl softened wafer over each cookie. Remove to wire racks to cool completely. Store in an airtight container.

Makes 3 dozen

GERMAN CHOCOLATE COOKIES

JASMINE CLIFTON
COLORADO SPRINGS, CO

I created these cookies for my father-in-law, who just loves German chocolate cake. Using cake mix to make cookies gives you big, soft cookies that are so good!

In a large bowl, combine dry cake mix, oil and eggs. Beat with an electric mixer on medium-high speed until thoroughly blended. Roll into one-inch balls; place one inch apart on baking sheets sprayed with non-stick vegetable spray. Bake at 350 degrees for about 8 minutes, until just starting to set. Immediately remove cookies to a wire rack. Spread with frosting when cool. Store in an airtight container.

18-1/4 oz. pkg. German chocolate cake mix
1/4 c. oil
3 eggs, beaten
14-1/2 oz. can coconut-pecan frosting

Makes 2 dozen

GRANDMOTHER'S APPLE CRUNCH

KAREN SYLVIA
BRIGHTON, CO

My sons love this yummy old-fashioned dessert! My grandmother used to make this delicious recipe in the fall and it has been handed down for two generations.

Place apples in an ungreased 8"x8" baking pan; set aside. In a bowl, mix remaining ingredients except ice cream. Sprinkle mixture over apples. Bake at 350 degrees for 30 minutes, or until apples are tender. Serve warm, topped with ice cream, if desired.

6 to 8 Granny Smith apples, cored, peeled and sliced
1/2 c. brown sugar, packed
1/2 c. sugar
1/2 c. all-purpose flour
1/2 c. butter, softened
cinnamon to taste
Optional: vanilla ice cream

Serves 6

SOUR CHERRY LATTICE PIE

SHARON DEMERS
DOLORES, CO

When I was little, my father would sing, "Can you bake a cherry pie, Sharon girl, Sharon girl?" and I would giggle and say "Nooo!" Well, now I can!

2 9-inch pie crusts, unbaked

4 c. sour cherries, pitted and 1/2 c. juice reserved

1 c. sugar

1 T. all-purpose flour

2-1/2 T. cornstarch

juice and zest of one lime

2 T. butter, diced

1 egg, beaten

2 T. whipping cream

Place one crust in a 9" pie plate. Wrap with plastic wrap; chill. Cut remaining crust into one-inch wide strips; cut leftover crust into star shapes with a cookie cutter. Place lattice strips and stars on a parchment paper-lined baking sheet; cover with plastic wrap and chill. Combine cherries and juice in a large bowl. Sprinkle with sugar, flour, cornstarch, lime juice and zest. Toss well and pour into pie crust; dot with butter. Weave lattice strips over filling. Arrange stars on lattice. Whisk together egg and cream; brush over crust. Bake at 400 degrees for about 50 minutes, until bubbly and crust is golden. Cool slightly before cutting.

Serves 6 to 8

KITCHEN TIP

A baker's secret! Grease muffin cups on the bottoms and just halfway up the sides. Muffins will bake up nicely puffed on top.

DARK CHOCOLATE PECAN PIE

RITA MORGAN
PUEBLO, CO

Decadent, rich and fantastic! My husband always saves room for dessert when this is on the menu.

In a bowl, stir together pecans, chocolate chips and flour; set aside. In another bowl, beat butter and brown sugar until well blended. Beat in eggs, one at a time. Mix in corn syrup, vanilla and salt, just until blended. Stir in pecan mixture. Pour into baked pie crust. Bake at 325 degrees for 55 to 60 minutes, until a toothpick inserted in center comes out with just melted chocolate. Center will set as it cools. Cool on a wire rack. Chill until serving time. Garnish with whipped topping.

Serves 8

1-1/2 c. pecan halves
1-1/2 c. dark chocolate chips
1 T. all-purpose flour
1/2 c. butter, softened
1/2 c. light brown sugar, packed
3 eggs
1/2 c. dark corn syrup
2 t. vanilla extract
1/4 t. salt
9-inch pie crust, baked
Garnish: whipped topping

PERFECT PUMPKIN–APPLE CAKE

SANDRA SULLIVAN
AURORA, CO

No oven needed...so easy to do on the run! This tasty cake is perfect for when your oven is all tied up with other yummy treats.

- 1/2 c. butter, softened
- 1-1/2 c. brown sugar, packed
- 1 c. canned pumpkin
- 3 eggs
- 2 c. all-purpose flour
- 2 t. baking powder
- 1/4 t. baking soda
- 1 t. cinnamon
- 1/4 t. salt
- Optional: chopped walnuts or pecans to taste
- 21-oz. can apple pie filling
- 12-oz. container frozen whipped topping, thawed

In a large bowl, beat together butter and brown sugar with an electric mixer on low speed until well mixed. Beat in pumpkin and eggs until blended. In a separate bowl, sift together flour, baking powder, baking soda, cinnamon and salt. Slowly add flour mixture to butter mixture; beat for 2 minutes. Fold in nuts, if using. Spoon pie filling into a slow cooker; pour batter over pie filling. Cover and cook on high setting for 1-1/2 to 2 hours, until a toothpick tests clean. Garnish servings with a dollop of whipped topping.

Serves 8

STICKY TOFFEE PUDDINGS

DENISE NEAL
CASTLE ROCK, CO

My husband and I first tried this dessert in a quaint village pub while on vacation in England. I just had to have the recipe so I could make it at home! I love the gooey sauce...sometimes I even double the toffee coating mixture to have more yummy topping with my dessert!

Blend butter and sugar well; stir in egg and set aside. Sift together flour and baking powder. Add gradually to butter mixture; mix well. Place dates in a bowl and pour boiling water over top; add baking soda and vanilla. Mix well and add to butter mixture. Pour into 6 greased 5" mini pie plates. Bake at 350 degrees for 30 minutes, or until puddings test done with a toothpick. Spoon Toffee Coating over hot puddings; place under broiler just until coating begins to bubble (careful, it burns easily!). Serve warm, topped with a dollop of whipped cream.

Serves 6

4 T. butter, softened

3/4 c. sugar

1 egg, beaten

1 c. all-purpose flour

1 t. baking powder

3/4 c. chopped dates

1-1/4 c. boiling water

1 t. baking soda

1 t. vanilla extract

Garnish: whipped cream

INDEX

Soups

U.S. to METRIC RECIPE EQUIVALENTS

Volume Measurements

¼ teaspoon. . . . . 1 mL
½ teaspoon. . . . . 2 mL
1 teaspoon . . . . 5 mL
1 tablespoon = 3 teaspoons. . . . . . 15 mL
2 tablespoons = 1 fluid ounce . . . . 30 mL
¼ cup. . . . . 60 mL
⅓ cup. . . . . 75 mL
½ cup = 4 fluid ounces. . . . . 125 mL
1 cup = 8 fluid ounces . . . . 250 mL
2 cups = 1 pint = 16 fluid ounces 500 mL
4 cups = 1 quart . . . . 1 L

Weights

1 ounce . . . . 30 g
4 ounces . . . . 120 g
8 ounces . . . . 225 g
16 ounces = 1 pound . . . . 450 g

Baking Pan Sizes

Square
8x8x2 inches . . . . 2 L = 20x20x5 cm
9x9x2 inches . . . . . . 2.5 L = 23x23x5 cm

Rectangular
13x9x2 inches . . . . . 3.5 L = 33x23x5 cm

Loaf
9x5x3 inches . . . . 2 L = 23x13x7 cm

Round
8x1½ inches . . . . 1.2 L = 20x4 cm
9x1½ inches . . . . 1.5 L = 23x4 cm

Recipe Abbreviations

t. = teaspoon. . . . . ltr. = liter
T. = tablespoon. . . . . . . .oz. = ounce
c. = cup. . . . . .lb. = pound
pt. = pint. . . . . .doz. = dozen
qt. = quart. . . . . .pkg. = package
gal. = gallon. . . . . .env. = envelope

Oven Temperatures

300° F. . . . . .150° C
325° F. . . . . .160° C
350° F. . . . . .180° C
375° F. . . . . .190° C
400° F. . . . . .200° C
450° F. . . . . .230° C

Kitchen Measurements

A pinch = ⅛ tablespoon
1 fluid ounce = 2 tablespoons
3 teaspoons = 1 tablespoon
4 fluid ounces = ½ cup
2 tablespoons = ⅛ cup
8 fluid ounces = 1 cup
4 tablespoons = ¼ cup
16 fluid ounces = 1 pint
8 tablespoons = ½ cup
32 fluid ounces = 1 quart
16 tablespoons = 1 cup
16 ounces net weight = 1 pound
2 cups = 1 pint
4 cups = 1 quart
4 quarts = 1 gallon

Send us your favorite recipe

and the memory that makes it special for you!*

If we select your recipe for a brand-new **Gooseberry Patch** cookbook, your name will appear right along with it...and you'll receive a FREE copy of the book!

Submit your recipe on our website at

www.gooseberrypatch.com/sharearecipe

*Please include the number of servings and all other necessary information.

Have a taste for more?

Visit www.gooseberrypatch.com to join our Circle of Friends!

• Free recipes, tips and ideas plus a complete cookbook index
• Get mouthwatering recipes and special email offers delivered to your inbox.

You'll also love these cookbooks from **Gooseberry Patch**!

5-Ingredient Family Favorite Recipes
America's Comfort Foods
Best Church Suppers
Best-Ever Cookie, Brownie & Bar Recipes
Best-Ever Sheet Pan & Skillet Recipes
Cozy Christmas Comforts
Delicious Recipes for Diabetics
Harvest Homestyle Meals
Healthy, Happy, Homemade Meals
Meals in Minutes: 15, 20, 30

www.gooseberrypatch.com